Journeys through Britain with a Pack Pony
1985 - 1987

Jane Dotchin

Journeys through Britain with a Pack Pony
1985 – 1987

by

Jane Dotchin

First published September 2021
Reprinted February 2024
Reprinted July 2025
by
Wagtail Press, Gairshield, Hexham
Northumberland
NE47 0HS

http://www.wagtailpress.uk

email: wagtailpress@yahoo.co.uk

Text and Illustrations
© Jane Dotchin

No reproduction permitted of any part of this book without prior arrangement with the author.

ISBN 978-0-9559395-7-0

Cover photograph by Guy Carpenter

CONTENTS

Foreword by HRH The Duchess of Cornwall

Introduction   1

1   Journey North to Dunoon   7
      with Sitka, Russet & Pippin

2   Journey South to Sussex   45
      with Sitka, Russet & Pippin

3   Journey North to Dalbeattie   71
      with Oriel, Russet & Tinker

4   Journey South to Devon   79
      with Sitka, Russet & Tinker

5   About Jane   106

Several years ago, I received a rather unusual parcel in the post: a handwritten letter from Jane Dotchin, accompanied by a copy of her diary of her recent pony trek. It was warm, witty and evocative, and illustrated beautifully by the author. She asked me if I would write a foreword for it. Her story was of particular interest to me as, whilst walking in Scotland, I had met Jane, her pony and her two Jack Russell Terriers (one in a saddle bag!) descending the Spittal path on her way to Ballater 'en route' to Inverness. I couldn't believe that at her great age, minus an eye, with only her four-legged friends for company she had covered hundreds of miles from her home in Northumberland to Inverness and back again... a feat for someone half her age!

Since then, Jane has sent me more of her diaries and I suggested that she should write a book about her intrepid experiences, as I was quite sure others would enjoy her stories as much as I do. So I'm delighted that "Journeys Through Britain With A Pack Pony 1985-1987" has now been published, and I hope it will be followed by this remarkable lady's further adventures...

Camilla

INTRODUCTION

"I'm afraid we're going to have to remove your eye," the doctor said.

"I've tried my best to repair it, but your sight is not coming back. If I don't take it out it could become infected which could pass to the other eye," he continued.

I had been in the eye hospital at Walkergate for over a week since being rushed there by ambulance: one of my cows tossed its head when I was tying it up and its horn had pierced my right eye.

It was July 1984 and we were having a beautiful summer. I certainly didn't want to be stuck in hospital at Walkergate of all places!

"We will operate after the weekend," the doctor told me.

"I suppose we must be thankful for small mercies," I replied. It was only last October I had a cataract removed from my left eye and the one in my right eye was due to be removed. There was no need to remove it now! The doctor smiled then said, "I'll see you next week," and off he went.

What was I going to do with myself while I was in hospital? As the sun was shining brilliantly I had to go outside. All the other patients were either bedridden or in the sitting area looking miserable. I tried walking into the town but the roar of traffic in the built-up area was a far cry from where I lived in Hexhamshire.

Then I got a message from home: did I need anything brought into hospital when they came to visit?

"Yes please, could you bring in my sketching pad and pens, then I can get the illustrations done for my book 'Journeys through England with a Pack Pony'."

With cataracts on both eyes, it had been difficult to see well enough to sketch. Once the left eye was free from blurred vision, I could see well but somehow I had never got round to getting those sketches done. Now was a good opportunity to make a start.

The nurses were very helpful. They found a table and chair and put them out in the small yard behind the ward so I could go outside, sit in the sun and sketch. While doing so I could relive the twelve journeys I had made down into the south of England with Sitka, the Haflinger stallion. I had bought him as a foal in 1966 after seeing this beautiful little bright chestnut creature with a flaxen mane and tail cantering around the field with his mother.

Sitka and I had made regular trips each spring to visit his breeder, Catherine Harbury, who lived near Dalbeattie in south west Scotland. We had already been this spring prior to my eye accident and seen Sitka's mother Lidia, with another colt foal. Catherine had already named him Jester because he was born on April 1st. He was to be Lidia's last foal because she was now 21 years old and was to retire from breeding.

The plan was to go back again in the autumn with Sitka when Jester would be six months old and ready to leave his mother. Sitka and I would stay with Catherine for one week and I would coax Jester away from his mum then get him halter broken. After a week a friend would come with her horsebox and take all three of us home; but of course, I hadn't planned to lose an eye and be in hospital, so Jester stayed where he was.

I had had to close my riding school in the autumn of 1983 to have the cataract operation and after only six months of getting back into riding school routine it had to be closed again.   Then there were my invalid parents to consider who were far from happy about the arrangements I had made to have them looked after while I was in hospital.

It wasn't long after the eye was removed that I was out of hospital and back at home again but with strict instructions not to do any heavy or strenuous work for several weeks.

By October, the eye socket was fully healed and I was free to get back to normal life, but before getting the riding school operating again, I would make that trip over to Catherine Harbury's again with Sitka and do as planned; halter breaking Jester.

Sitka was eighteen years old now and was suffering from a cancerous growth that was affecting his 'waterworks'. The vet wasn't too sure how long he could continue on before the situation got too bad and there would be no alternative but to have him put to sleep.

He would now only be carrying saddle bags and Russet, my terrier, who rode in one of the saddle bags when he was tired or when we were on roads and it was too dangerous to have a dog running loose. I no longer expected him to carry me as well so I would be leading him all the way.

We were not far into October when Sitka, Russet and I set out for Kielder Forest to stay with my aunt who lived in a cottage north of Kielder village.

After a night with my aunt, we headed west over to Langholm then on past Dumfries to Dalbeattie and to Catherine's lovely bungalow overlooking the Solway Firth. Jester and his mother were running out with other ponies on thirty acres of rough moorland covered with a variety of trees and bushes. It could take half an hour or more to find them all. It was going to be too risky to take Sitka into the area where they were so I tied him up outside the gate.

Once I found all the ponies, they followed me back to the gate, saw Sitka and then curiosity had them all peering over the gate with young Jester making sure he got the best view of this new arrival.

Next morning, they all met me at the gate as soon as they saw Sitka. With Catherine's help we managed to entice Jester through the gate without any of the others following. I then led Sitka to a nearby cattle shed with Jester following him where they would be company for each other.

Whether Jester knew he was with his very much older brother or not, I don't know but there seemed to be some kind of instinctive bond between them.

After giving Jester his daily leading lesson, I started 'breaking in' one of Catherine's Haflinger x Norwegian mares who was now four years old and ready to learn to be ridden. It didn't take long to get her going forward on long reins with saddle and bridle on. Next was getting on to her back.

Having led Sitka all the way to Dalbeattie I hadn't been on horseback since losing an eye. It took a bit of adapting to at first, but I hadn't realised how much it would affect my balance when riding. Toscina, as the mare was called, let me mount her and seemed to accept my instructions to move forward so we practised going round the yard moving forward then stopping, counting five, then moving forward again. As she was doing so well, I decided to take her out along the nearby farm track. She stepped out well for a while. Then she stopped dead, ears pricked, eyes alert and stood, refusing to go forward. The more I urged her on, the more she refused. Then suddenly she spun round and was ready to bolt back the way she had come. We had quite a tussle. I was determined not to let her bolt off but was finding great difficulty keeping my balance. It became quite a challenge for both of us. I knew I had to win or Toscina's education would be badly marred. It took a good half hour of struggling and it made me realise that two eyes are better than one!

When it came time to go home again, Catherine and I wondered how we would get Jester into the horsebox, but we need not have worried. He followed big brother up the ramp and into the horsebox without hesitation and off we went back towards Hexham.

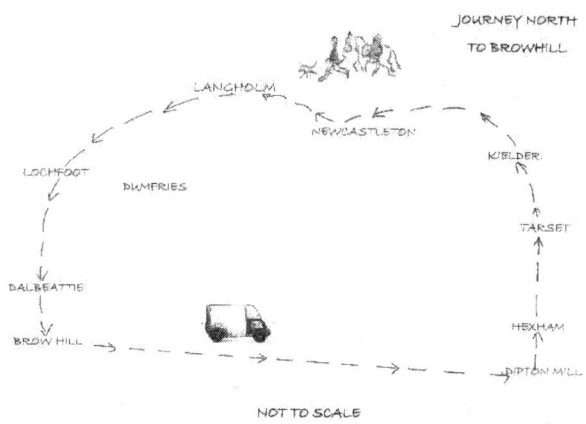

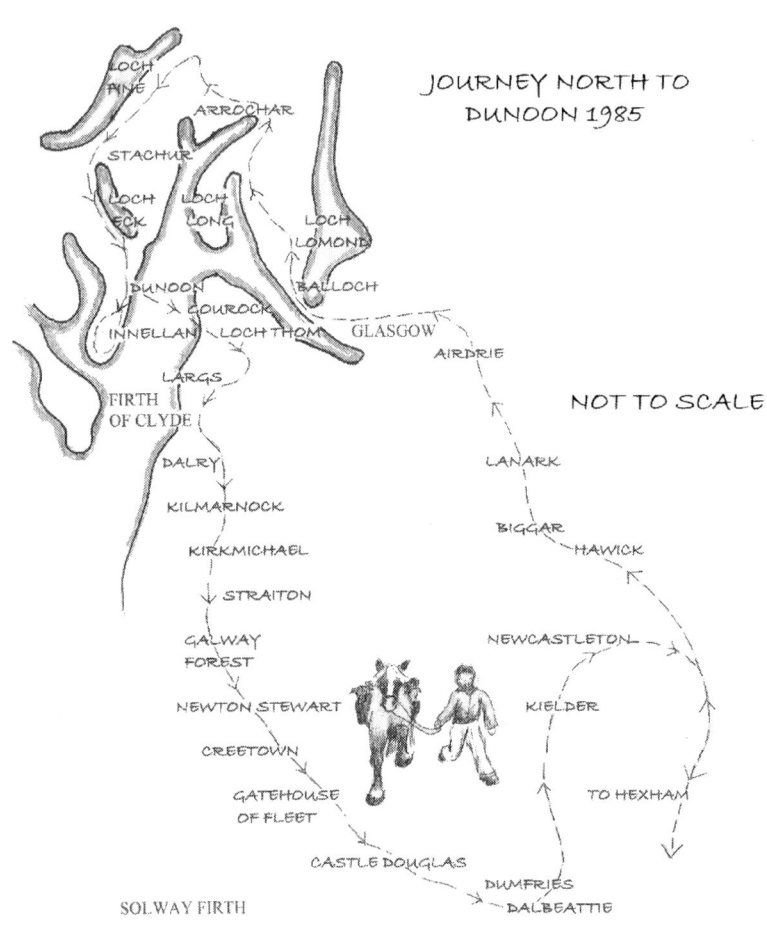

1

JOURNEY NORTH TO DUNOON WITH SITKA, RUSSET & PIPPIN

September 1985

Jester grew rapidly. He was going to be bigger than his brother but it was going to be a few years before he could take over the role of a pack pony.

Sitka was back to being a riding school pony knowing the routine well, carrying many a young inexperienced rider as if they were in control, yet really it was he who knew what he should be doing.

That horrible growth that was causing problems with his 'water works' had not got much worse so by September 1985 I planned to take him with Russet up north to meet friends near Dunoon in Scotland. Jester was quite happy running out with the other ponies so he could be with them while I took Sitka away for a few weeks.

Some weeks before setting off I was taking some children for a riding lesson and Russet was rabbiting nearby down a bank alongside the field we were riding in. I expected him to join us again as he usually did when we went back to the stables. This time he never appeared. Once everyone had gone home and the ponies were turned out in the field, I went to look for him but he never arrived however much I shouted and called. Night time came, still no sign of Russet.

A week went by and still no Russet.

The bank was a mass of rabbit burrows. Various friends helped me by digging into each one but it was useless. We kept getting to a tangle of tree roots as we dug and still no sign of Russet.

I couldn't be without a dog so when an advert in the local paper said 'Jack Russell puppies for sale' Off I went to look at them and came home with a lovely little seven-week-old Jack Russell bitch. With this tiny little handful of adorable piddling puppy, I was able to keep my mind away from what had happened to Russet and stop worrying about him suffering stuck down a rabbit hole. He couldn't possibly be alive after all this time.

Back in the same field taking some children for a riding lesson, one of them said "Where's Russet?" They were all used to him always being near us. I explained how he had disappeared and I suspected he had got trapped down a rabbit hole. Suddenly all the children shouted at the top of their voices "Russet, RUSSET, where are you?" A few minutes later, one child said "Look, there he is!" and pointed towards the bank at the edge of the field.

I looked in amazement. There was this skinny little soiled creature walking towards us. Was it Russet? I wasn't sure. Then as I got nearer, I realised it was Russet. His ribs were sticking out, his coat was matted with soil and what looked worse were his eyes. His head had shrunk so his eyes seemed to bulge out of his skull. He must have heard the children shouting his name and then tried to move and realised he was so thin he could get himself out of where he was stuck. After several days of careful feeding, he recovered and was back to his energetic self.

Now I had two terriers to put into Sitka's saddle bags for our trip to Dunoon. I had an old ex-Army nose bag which must have been Army surplus horse equipment; I had bought this heavy canvas nosebag with some other ex-Army bits and pieces back in 1962 when starting up the riding school.

After Russet's return from his rabbit hole trauma and he had regained his strength again, I would pop his new little Jack Russell companion in the nosebag and sling it over my shoulder then take Russet for a walk. Pippin would curl up in the bottom of the nosebag and go fast asleep as she was well used to being carried. I could see no problem in getting her used to being in a saddlebag on Sitka, but I could see a problem over balance.

Russet was twice the size of Pippin and possibly over twice the weight. If I had one on each side of Sitka in front of the saddle, Russet's weight would pull the saddle over. So, the saddle bag Pippin was in had to have an extra compartment added underneath just big enough to put the spare set of horseshoes in. As soon as Russet saw me begin to get the saddle bags ready, he began to get excited. Pippin, sensing his excitement, bounced around annoying him.

When we did eventually set off across the fields, Russet raced ahead with Pippin running after him. By the time we got to the track through the woods, Pippin had had enough so I picked her up and put her in her saddlebag.

It was many years now since I had ridden a very lively Haflinger stallion down to Somerset. Sitka was now nineteen years old and a very placid gelding who had no intention of hurrying as we walked along. The slow rhythm of his stride soon had Pippin fast asleep.

After a few miles we had to go onto a tarmac road so I lifted Russet up into his saddlebag opposite the sleeping Pippin. A few minutes later I heard growling behind me as I led Sitka. I turned round to find Pippin had crawled out of her saddlebag and was up Sitka's neck tugging at his mane growling as if she had caught a rabbit and was trying to kill it.

I pushed her back in her saddlebag and fastened her firmly in then on we went. It wasn't long before I heard more growling and turned round to see what was happening this time. It was Russet who was disagreeing with Pippin's antics. Her head was still fastened to her saddlebag but she had managed to get her bottom out so was hanging there with her back legs on the saddle and her bum in the air annoying Russet.

Eventually we managed to get on the next bridleway so both terriers could get out of their saddlebags and have a run. Russet was racing about chasing rabbits and Pippin was running as fast as she could chasing Russet. After that, Pippin was tired and sat in her saddlebag sleeping most of the rest of the journey to our first camp in Kielder Forest.

Once I had the tent up both terriers curled up asleep on Sitka's saddle blanket. We were to stay with my Aunt Belle the next night in her cottage just north of Kielder village which was only half a day's journey from where we were camping. No need to have an early start. We could just take our time in the morning. Pippin was only a few months old and she would be tired.

It wasn't even daylight when I suddenly woke feeling this wet thing on my face and something crawling all over my head. It was a very wide-awake Pippin licking me then bouncing around on my sleeping bag, before attacking my face again with that tongue. I tried to get her to settle down again so we could wait for daylight but it didn't really work. She was not going to sleep again so annoyed Russet instead. He growled at her so she bounced back onto my sleeping bag then tried to lick my face again.

I unzipped the tent to see if it was light enough to get moving. Sitka was standing just beside us. Suddenly Pippin shot out of the tent, rushed towards Sitka ,grabbed his tail and swung on it, refusing to let go as Sitka moved forward in surprise. He then stopped, turned around and looked at this little body hanging off his tail then decided to stand and wait till it let go.

We got to Aunt Belle's soon after lunchtime. She had a chocolate-coloured Labrador called Rory. Pippin wasn't too sure of this big dog. He looked rather large and frightening but when Aunt Belle produced a bowl of food for all three dogs, Pippin decided she would have Rory's large bowl of food and he could have her small one. So, she pushed him away from his bowl and told him plainly it was to be hers.

Most of our route the next day was on Forestry tracks through to Newcastleton. Unless there were Forestry operations going on in the forest, we could be free from traffic, so neither terrier needed to be in their saddlebag for several miles. Every so often, Pippin would be so tired I would pick her up and put her in her saddlebag and she would sleep for a while. I kept turning round to see if she was still asleep, then when finding she had woken up and was crawling up Sitka's neck or balancing on the packs, I would let her down to run for a while until she was exhausted and needing to be lifted back into her saddlebag for another rest. Like all puppies, energy comes in sudden bursts, followed by going to sleep before the next burst of energy.

Putting the tent up that night north of Newcastleton both terriers were so tired. Russet sat head hanging down waiting for the saddle blanket to go into the tent so he could get inside and lie on it. Pippin decided she couldn't wait so got onto my rolled up sleeping bag on the grass, curled up on it and went fast asleep.

England has rights of way signposted as 'public footpaths' and 'bridleways' with different markings on OS maps so one knows which is which; bridleways are suitable for going along with a horse, no stiles or kissing gates etc. Scottish tracks on the OS maps are all marked the same and back then there was no guarantee a right of way would be open and not be fenced off or have a locked gate across it or a stile not suitable for a horse to pass through.

I had tried two tracks marked on the map, to avoid being on the road through the central belt area, and both were blocked by a barbed wire fence so we had to go back and round by road. The next few days were pretty well all on roads and some awfully busy ones.

We were on one quiet narrow road one day and I was just about to let both terriers out of their saddle bags for a bit when I heard the roar of a very fast car approaching from behind us. We were coming to a sharp bend in the road and there was already a car slowing down behind us waiting to see if the road ahead was clear, when the roar of the fast vehicle came at an alarming speed, overtaking the car behind us and passed us right on the sharp bend when a car came the other way.

There was a sudden crash and a squeal of brakes and smell of burning rubber. Both cars had smashed in bonnets but the driver of the speeding car slammed his gears into reverse then shot forward and made for the gap between us and the car he had knocked into. I only just managed to haul Sitka into the side and avoid being hit. The driver of the car that had been waiting behind us got out of his vehicle and went to see if the person in the hit car was alright. I got Sitka round the bend ahead quickly before another vehicle came. We were all suffering from shock. Fortunately, the person in the crashed into vehicle was alright but his car was far from it. The man from the car that had slowed down behind us seemed to be seeing to the situation so we walked on but I made sure both terriers stayed in their saddlebags.

Where could I let both of them have a run? They couldn't stay in the saddlebags all day and it looked as if we were going to have to stay on roads for a lot more miles in this busy area. We came to an open gateway into an area of rough grass. Surely nobody would mind if we went in there to stop and have our lunch? I reasoned. So, we went in until we got well off the road then I let Sitka graze, took both terriers out of their saddlebags and we sat down to have the bread and cheese I had put ready for us before we set off early in the morning.

Russet knew well the routine at picnic time and it didn't take Pippin long to learn it; a large mouthful of bread and cheese for me, a smaller one for Russet and an even smaller one for Pippin! Both terriers would sit in front of me waiting their turn. After bread and cheese out came the bottle of milk and each terrier had a drink out of my pan then, provided there was no rain and no strong wind, I would get out my camping Gaz stove and brew up for myself a full pan of coffee while the two terriers had a wander round.

All three of us finished the bread and cheese this time and I had managed to brew up the coffee, so was sitting back enjoying it when I suddenly realised there was no terrier in site. Horrors; we weren't that far from the road; where were they? No sign of them towards the road, but where were they? Then away in the other direction across the fields I saw Russet racing after what I thought was a hare and away behind him was a little white dot running for all she was worth after him. I watched as the hare gained speed and Russet got left further and further behind, then he gave up and I could see him heading back towards me.

A very puffed Russet arrived back beside me and lay down panting, but where was Pippin? We waited and waited but no Pippin. Then suddenly there was this agonising cry in the distance. Again and again this piercing cry. What was it? Was it Pippin? Was she hurt? Maybe she was caught in one of those awful gin traps or a snare? I ran off across the field and the frantic yells got louder and louder. I came to a ditch with a steep bank on the other side then a thick hedge which looked impossible to get over. The yells seemed to come from the other side of it. How could I get there? Eventually I found a gap I could crawl through and there about a hundred yards to my left was Pippin sitting with her head in the air yelling for all she was worth. I shouted "Pippin!" and she jumped up and came racing towards me, now with yells of delight; she was so pleased to see me. There was no mark on her, she was only totally lost and the cries were cries of despair. I picked her up and she wriggled with excitement and cries of delight at being rescued as I carried her back to where we had left Sitka grazing with Russet lying beside him.

We were now north of Langholm after a horrid journey through the town with its awfully busy road with huge trucks belching fumes at us as we tried to keep on the pavement to avoid being squashed on the narrow main road. My map showed a track over the hillside in the direction we wanted to go. The alternative was a long way round by road. Did I dare risk trying that track? I could see it winding up to the skyline. It looked alright and being open hillside maybe there were no fences across it. Yes, we would try it.

To start with it was good until we came to a cottage. After that I could see where it wound its way up the hill so we climbed on up. Looking at my map it followed alongside a stream but as we got higher up it was obvious the stream had cut into its banks on each side and eroded the track causing deep gullies. We managed to clamber down the gullies and up the other side to join the track again, until we came to an extra deep one. I climbed down expecting Sitka to follow me. There was water at the bottom and I could see him preparing to jump so let go of the lead rein and got myself out of the way in case he jumped on me. With a huge leap he got himself across but as his hind legs landed on the bank it suddenly gave way. He had the weight of all the packs on his back, which seemed to pull him backwards and he landed on his back at the bottom of the gully.

I gasped in horror. He didn't move. Was he hurt? Could he move? I called "Sitka!" and he tried to struggle but couldn't make it. I climbed down the gully. I would have to try to relieve him of all the packs but that meant undoing various straps, which would mean getting right next to him. If he started to struggle again flinging his legs about, I could end

up damaged but I had to do something. "Lie still old fellow. Let me see what I can undo to relieve you of all these packs." He seemed to understand what I was trying to do and lay motionless.

I got the whole lot undone eventually and climbed out of the way then called "Come on Sitka. Up you get!" With a tremendous heave he got himself up and out of the gully leaving all the packs lying in the water below.

The poor fellow stood shivering; he was so traumatised. I climbed down and heaved various bits of equipment, dripping with muddy water, up the bank. It took several sessions of hauling wet things up the bank and dumping them beside Sitka.

He eventually looked calmer and stopped shivering and seemed to be alright, so I loaded it all on him again. Russet was sitting watching but Pippin was really upset and frightened by the whole episode. Once all was loaded on to Sitka and he walked forward again she looked relieved and cautiously followed after us.

The track improved as we got higher up the hillside. We came to an ancient old iron gate with a stone beside it with carved writing on it. I couldn't make out what it said as it was too weather-beaten and faint but I suspected we were on an old drove road, which hadn't been used for years.

Once through the gate the track wound its way back down into the valley below. The countryside was beautiful in brilliant sunshine. As we got lower, I was relieved to see tractor tyre marks on it. If a tractor can get down to the valley below, then so could we. We found a place to camp that night, as the sun went down the moon shone. It was a brilliant moon lit night. Maybe we're in for a dry spell, I thought. It had been a terrible wet summer. Farmers had struggled to get silage in. The ground was so wet with mud getting into the cut grass as tractors sank into the ground. Surely, we were due for a dry spell?

Next morning, rain beat on the tent getting heavier and heavier. Russet made no attempt to get up but Pippin and I both needed to go out. I unzipped the tent opening and peered out. We both felt like holding on, like Russet, but decided we couldn't so made a dash for it.

Pippin was back in the tent first and straight on my sleeping bag with her wet feet, having missed the dog towel I put out to catch her feet as she came in again. It was hard to believe the rain could get even heavier but it did and beat so hard the tent was sagging. Will it ever stop raining? We waited and waited and still the rain beat down. When eventually it eased, I managed to load up Sitka, ready to move on. Neither terrier looked at all enthusiastic.

We hadn't gone far when down came the rain again. After three hours in heavy rain, we began to feel we had had enough. If only we could find a shed to shelter inside and have our bread and cheese. Then we came to a cottage with a shed with a tin roof beside it. I called at the cottage but it all looked shut up and nobody answered my knocking at the door, so

we went into the shed while Sitka grazed the grass alongside with his waterproof sheet over him. .

After we had sat for a while, I could see both terriers felt as I did; that damp chill that penetrates when sitting in wet things so we moved on after dragging Sitka away from the good grass.

After another three hours in pouring rain, we had had enough. The wind had got up as well so the rain was driving straight at us. I would look for a farm in a sheltered place and ask if we could camp.

There ahead of us in a dip at the side of the road was a farmhouse. I led Sitka towards the door and knocked. A lady came to the door "Camp in this weather? You're welcome to a spare bed in the house. Put your pony in the field over there and come inside" she said. I lifted back the waterproof sheet on Sitka and revealed two terriers in their saddlebags. "Well, I've never seen that before. They do look comfortable in there and the little one looks very young."

Pippin was wriggling with excitement and trying desperately to get out of her saddlebag to say hello. With all the packs unloaded into an outside shed by the house, I put Sitka in the field. He looked at me and I could tell by the look on his face he was telling me the grass was not as good as he would like.

As we entered the house there was a poodle sitting staring at us. Pippin stood staring at it trying to work out whether she should be frightened or pleased to see him. Her tail wagged as she went nearer to him. Then she stopped motionless for a while. Soon the stumpy tail began to wag then with a sudden dart she shot up to him and unfortunately grabbed one of his floppy ears and tugged at it. He yelped and she let go.

I could see Russet looking at me with a sideways glance. He had seen a comfortable chair and wanted to jump up onto it. It looked as if the poodle had been on it, so when I didn't say no he jumped up on it and made himself comfortable. I knew well if I had said no he would have waited until no one was looking and got on it anyway. Even if it had been some best clean armchair and I had said "Russet down!" somehow he always got away with it as the owner would say "Oh leave him, he looks so comfortable!."

My host said she was going to be off early in the morning as she was off to Devon and needed to make a very early start. So, I got up around 6 am and went out to get Sitka and give him his oats then get him ready. I went back to the house around 7am, but no sign of my host. By 7.30am the poodle turned up and Pippin had a good game of 'catch my ears if you can' with Pippin racing after him. We set off about 8, but we seemed to be far from ready for that early start to Devon.

It wasn't raining, but the wet still on the roads was getting sprayed up over us by thoughtless speeding drivers making Sitka very nervous after the two cars crashed beside him back in Biggar.

There was no way of avoiding roads today. Fortunately, Pippin's romping around with the poodle had her tired so no wriggling out of her saddlebag. She had her nose tucked into it and slept most of the way. A farmer let us camp on a level patch up a bank near the entrance to his farm that night. It was the only area he could suggest that didn't have water oozing out of the ground when you trod on it. There was just room for the tent and to tether Sitka so he could get enough grass.

All seemed so cold and damp so we were all three of us pleased to get into the tent.

It was a long trudge again in the rain the next day; Both terriers were quite happy to stay in their saddlebags under the waterproof sheet over all the packs.

It was hard to persuade Pippin to relieve herself before getting into the tent once I got it up as the rain continued to pour down. Russet knew

the routine; a quick pee then a good shake to get rid of all the wet on his coat then dive into the tent. Every time I hauled Pippin out to do a pee she dashed back in again as soon as I put her down on the wet grass. So, I gave up until later hoping there would be no puddle in the tent.

Later as Russet and I were drifting off to sleep, Pippin decided she really wasn't tired at all; she had done plenty sleeping in her saddlebag. At first, she started to annoy Russet hoping he would play with her but he would have none of it. So, she started leaping up at me trying to catch my hair. Then she found a toggle on the top of my sleeping bag; tugging and pulling it, leaping up and down, growling louder and louder as the game got more and more exciting. Russet got more annoyed so started growling at her but she thought that was part of the game and he was joining in, until exasperated, Russet leapt up and snapped at her.

That quietened her down for a few minutes, but soon she was back to what was left of the toggle and started tugging at it again. As soon as I started scolding her, she thought it was part of the game. It was hopeless. Then I remembered the chews I put in the saddlebags and had forgotten all about. So, I got them out and gave her one. That did the trick. She settled down afterwards and we all got some sleep.

In the morning I turned on my pocket radio to hear the forecast. Oh no - yet more rain! Another wet day but by afternoon it cleared up and the sun came out. We were on a quiet road so I let both the terriers out of their saddlebags and they bounced on ahead of me full of energy. Suddenly they both leapt into the verge and up to a stone wall by a tree and barked frantically. What had they found? As Sitka and I caught up with them I saw that they were leaping up and down at a tree. The trunk divided a few feet up and in the middle was a cow's head. It was absolutely wedged between the divided trunk. I got my hands underneath its head but it was stuck fast. All it did was roll its eyes and make strange gurgling noises as if it was about to choke. What else could I do to free it?

There was no farm in sight so I tried again and got my hands under its head and heaved. This time it started to panic and its back legs were starting to crash about and the gurgling noises got worse so I stood back to see if it would quieten down. One more try?

Pippin thought it was a great game leaping up trying to catch a cow's head stuck in a tree. Even Russet joined in this time so the game got really exciting. I pulled them away to let the cow calm down and the gurgling noises stopped. Again – one more try?

So, I let go of both dogs and quickly got both hands under the cow's jaw and heaved – Wow – it's free! Its head shot backwards and the whole beast fell back then off it went down the field and stopped to graze as if nothing had happened.

Will it ever stop raining, I kept thinking, as we plodded on day after day in the wet. There were fine intervals at times but they were few and usually in the mornings, then by afternoon it became continuous heavy rain. We were heading towards Helensburgh and had come through Balloch which was full of Loch Lomond tourists who got excited with their cameras at the sight of a pack pony with two terriers in saddlebags; Pippin got excited by all the attention and attempted to wriggle out of her saddlebag to say hello to everyone.

We were able to stay on the old main road from Balloch but had to go on to the terribly busy new main road for a couple of miles before turning off onto the Helensburgh road. It was two miles of hell with huge speeding vehicles flying past us. Every time we tried to get off the road and into the side, branches kept catching into the saddlebags. Poor Sitka was terrified and so was I.

From the Helensburgh road we turned off onto a lovely quiet road to Glen Fruin. It was so peaceful after all that traffic. I could let Russet and Pippin out of their saddlebags; they were so pleased to be free to run ahead – even in the rain. Pippin decided it was too boring just to run ahead and decided it would be far more exciting catching hold of the hair on Sitka's fetlocks. It was far too dangerous so I yelled "No!" at her. That was fine for a while but then she decided to have another try at catching one of those fetlocks.

There was a sudden yelp as one of Sitka's front hooves had caught her toe. She cried in agony then ran into the ditch not really knowing where to put herself as she was in so much pain. I picked her up and saw two of her claws had been broken off and her foot was bleeding. Sitka was most upset at the cries of distress and nuzzled her with his nose as I held her.

Eventually back in her saddlebag she went to sleep, then once in the tent that night she made it obvious she was much better when she started frisking about just as Russet wanted to go to sleep. Out came the chews again then after a while she settled down and we all three could sleep. I only wished Sitka could be in the tent with us as rain beat down on us yet again.

Next morning it was still pouring with rain. The three of us pretended it was still night time as it was so dark and so wet. After a while Pippin and I had to venture out. Russet had no intention of joining us. It was a quick pee and quickly back to the tent. Poor Sitka was standing hunched up with his back to the driving rain. We did eventually get started as the rain eased but we hadn't gone far when it got heavier again.

We were passing a cottage when a voice called out "Would you like to come in and have a cup of coffee?" I could just see a figure standing in the open doorway of the cottage. At the sound of a strange voice Pippin's nose peered out from underneath the waterproof cover on Sitka, then Russet pushed his head out and a loud laugh came from the lady standing in the doorway. "Bring the dogs in as well."

I tied Sitka up where he could get some grass then Russet, Pippin and I went in and sat beside a lovely fire and I was handed a welcome mug of coffee. As we were chatting the lady's husband joined us. I thought it might be worth asking if they knew of any tracks in the area where we could go through and avoid roads. "Can't you just ride up over the hill?" he said. It never seemed to occur to him that there could be bogs, fences or even locked gates.

It was hard to leave that nice warm fire and go out into the rain again. I had to carry Pippin and call Russet to follow us several times before he would move. Sitka had finished the patch of grass where he had been tied up and gave a welcome neigh as we came outside. With both dogs in the saddlebags we waved goodbye to our hosts and continued along the Glen Fruin road through picturesque but wet countryside.

It was getting late as we got near Portincaple by Loch Long when a car passed us then turned into an opening ahead of us. An elderly couple got out of their car and the lady stopped to wait for me then began to chat and ask where we were going. She then led me down a winding path to the shore of the loch and said we were welcome to camp there. By then the rain had stopped and the hills stood out clearly. All looked really beautiful and we couldn't have found a more peaceful place to camp.

Once the tent was up it got too cold to linger outside admiring the view across the loch. Sitka was happily grazing as the grass was so good. The dogs and I had just got into the tent when the roar of an engine spoiled the quietness. Next, I heard Sitka charging about on the end of his tethering rope. Something had really upset him. I rushed out of the tent and there on the loch coming right towards us was a powerboat. I suspected whoever was in it had come to see what was on the shore. It suddenly turned as it got nearer to us and sped off with a woosh of water and roar of its engine and left Sitka standing shaking as he stared at it, obviously relieved it wasn't coming any nearer.

After that beautiful evening it was back to rain as we went on up the road to Arrochar. There were no more beautiful views over the loch; not only was there mist but also barricades along the shore as it was an Army Defence Area.

There was a good shop at Arrochar so I could stock up with carrots, porridge oats, milk and dog food. Unfortunately, there were no dog chews. The supply I had was getting low. Could Russet and I survive those energetic outbursts of Pippin in the evenings in the tent without them? Her paw was still sore. She limped when she was out of the saddlebag so rode most of the way but it never seemed to bother her once in the tent.

Up past Arrochar with its beach of washed-up litter which had collected at the end of the loch, we then made our way up past the Rest and Be Thankful viewpoint where we could turn off the main road for a while.

It was later that evening near Lochgoilhead I met my first unfriendly Scottish farmer. I had knocked on the farmhouse door and was greeted with an angry glowering face then when I asked if there was anywhere I might camp for the night I was told in no uncertain terms that I could not camp. I found myself apologising for asking and dragged Sitka away as quickly as possible.

We continued on as it got darker, Sitka getting slower and slower as he knew it was well past the time we should be stopping. We came to a wood alongside the road. Suddenly Sitka dragged me into an opening into the wood. I looked and there was a lovely sheltered grassy area ideal for putting up a tent and tethering a hungry pack pony.

It was another morning when I just wanted to stay in my sleeping bag and not face the day. Rain was pouring down and daylight seemed to have been washed away. Just as I was thinking how lovely and warm I was, I felt a wet tongue licking my face. I stuck my hand out to try and stop it but that seemed to be taken as a time for a game of bouncing on my hand then running over Russet and bouncing back to see if I would play a game of 'Catch Me If You Can!' I reached for the saddlebag for a chew – only two left now. I gave one to Pippin but she wasn't interested in it. She wanted to do something far more energetic than chewing.

We left our comfortable camping spot between the trees and made our way up Hell's Glen in mist and rain. It was so mild I decided to take off my waterproof hood and just let my hair get wet. It needed washing badly; my head felt all itchy.

Once my hair got really wet, I got out the small bottle of shampoo from the saddlebag and rubbed some into the wet hair. Later the rain stopped and the sun got out, so I stopped by a stream, got my camping pan and filled it from the stream and gave my hair a good rinse. It did feel better.

Next day we were plodding down the main road towards Strachur in yet more rain when a car pulled up alongside us and stopped. A man got out "Would you like somewhere to camp?" he said, then continued to explain that he had a caravan parked next to his house and plenty of grazing around about for a pony, just past Strachur. "Come and have a look and see what you think." Then he explained exactly where it was and left us. His directions led us to a small cottage up a lane off a back road out of the village. He had left his car at the end of the lane so that I would recognise it and know that we had come to the right place. He saw us approaching and came down the lane to meet us, then led us to the caravan parked by some trees beyond the cottage. He opened the caravan door for me to look inside then apologised for the oats spilled on the floor. "I use the caravan to store the goat's food and the sack of corn split when I went in to light the stove before you arrived," he explained.

Russet and I saw the warm glow from the stove as Sitka's nose came in the doorway having smelled the oats. Pippin had her eyes on the two goats that came to join us. She wasn't too sure whether to be frightened or not then decided she was frightened, so came running up to me to be picked up. Russet was by then in the caravan sitting by the stove. I put Pippin in the caravan while I unloaded the packs off Sitka. He licked up as much spilt oats as he could reach, stretching his head right into the caravan doorway. As I put all the wet packs in the caravan, I saw Pippin creep nearer the stove and get between it and Russet. Suddenly Russet realised she was getting all the heat and went for Pippin. I rushed up to grab him and picked up Pippin and plonked them both side by side and told them not to move while I sorted out all the wet things. The caravan looked like a cluttered drying room with every available spot having something hanging from it.

There was a knock on the caravan door and my host came with an armful of logs so I could keep the stove burning all night. He sat down and chatted about how as a young man he had been struck with a severe heart attack and as he was lying in hospital, he had taken a hard look at life and decided that he didn't want to die. After many months in hospital struggling to fully recover, he was eventually able to come home and live a reasonably normal life again. It had made him really appreciate life in a way he had never done before.

It reminded me of Geoff who I'd met with Sitka and Russet on the way to the ferry from Liverpool to the Isle of Man in 1983. Geoff had been trapped under a wagon he was repairing and no one realised he was there. The vehicle was driven off with Geoff trapped underneath the axle and when he was found he was given up for dead, but survived and realised how grateful he was for life and all it gave him.

Most of us live wanting more and more and have little time to appreciate what we have. Perhaps it isn't until we're faced with everything, including the threat of having one's life taken away from us, that we can really see the value of what we have.

I had arranged to meet some friends who were staying in an hotel in Dunoon in a couple of days, so hoped to find a good place nearby to camp.

We got into Dunoon and I tied Sitka up outside some shops then went to get some provisions and necessary dog chews. A man in white overalls came running out of the butcher's shop, kindly handed me a bag and said, "A bag of bones for your dogs!" then ran back to the butcher's shop.

After looking to see where the hotel was where I had arranged to meet my friends, I then enquired about the possible places I could camp for a few days and was directed to a farm on the outskirts of the town. We found the farm and yes, we were welcome to camp there as long as we liked.

For once, it wasn't raining as I put the tent up and tethered Sitka. The dogs lay in the grass chewing the bones. That kept them occupied for a couple of hours and got Pippin tired enough to settle down that night without her evening burst of energy.

Next morning the sun shone. Lovely, I thought. Let's just sit in the sun and rest.

"No!" said Pippin and she bounced around Russet annoying him then decided to annoy Sitka. So I decided to go for a walk up the hill behind us then perhaps she would settle down and rest in the sun. We set off leaving Sitka on his tether but he got so upset at being left behind I decided to let him follow us, but when we got to the track up the hill, he led the way with the two terriers following him and I was left puffing behind them. The view over the harbour and across the sea was fantastic. We sat on the hill top for a while, then scrambled back to our camping spot and were able to sit in peace in the sun by the tent.

We repeated the same the walk the next day and again the sun came out. I had kept the rest of the bones hidden from the dogs to give them the following day when I was going to leave them and go into Dunoon. Fortunately, it was another fine day, so I could tie them with their bones so there would be no quarrelling. Also, I didn't fancy greasy raw bones chewed inside the tent.

There were yells of excitement from Pippin when I returned from Dunoon. We sat together in the sun until dark clouds arrived and down came the rain so we rushed into the tent for shelter but I knew we needed to have a walk. Pippin would be far too full of energy if we didn't. So, with two reluctant terriers, we set off across the field in the rain, Russet walking behind me and Pippin trailing behind, but I was last into the tent when we got back.

My plan was to get the ferry across to Gourock then make our way down to Dumfriesshire to stay with Catherine near Dalbeattie before going home. I assumed I could just lead Sitka onto the ferry but 'No! The pony has to be in a horse trailer.' It took a long time to find anyone with a trailer who would take us, but eventually I was directed to the landlord of the pub in the main street of Dunoon. Yes, he could take us, but he was so busy he couldn't take us for two days.

I decided that as we had two days to spare we would go down the coast to Toward Point and then round the peninsula to where the road ends at Finnast Point. Then, I was told, a track would take us alongsde Loch Striven and eventually come out at Ardtaraig where we could join the road that would take us down Glen Lean, then onto the road back to Dunoon in time for the ferry crossing.

We set off through Dunoon with all its hotels and guest houses then down the coast towards Innellan. The weather was beautiful, so after several hours we stopped and sat in the sun.

After a couple of hours, Pippin had had enough and began to annoy Russet, then me, then Sitka, so we had to get going again. We camped that evening on the shore of Loch Striven. It was beautifully calm and peaceful. Lights from the Isle of Bute shone to the left of us across the water. Just the sound of water trickling down a nearby stream could be heard as I lay in the tent with two tired terriers asleep on the end of my sleeping bag.

It was disappointing waking up to thick mist. We couldn't see for two metres in front of us as we continued along the shore road.

We came to a very rickety bridge over a stream, which didn't look at all safe or strong enough to carry a pack pony. Sitka looked at it and snorted. I think he possibly remembered the bridge in Holwick in Teesside made of old railway sleepers across a metal frame. As we crossed it one of the sleepers gave way and fell in the water below leaving Sitka with one leg hanging through the gap. He had an awful struggle to get his hind leg back up and was lucky not to have broken it. We both got a horrid fright. This bridge looked as if it would all give way if Sitka got onto it. No, we would have to turn back as it was too risky and we needed to be sure of being in time for the ferry to Gourock.

The mist lifted and we picnicked in that lovely spot where we had camped, then got back to Port Lamont and called at the farm to see if we could get through the Corcarach Forest on a track marked on the map. Yes, we could but we might have to call at the cottage on the edge of the forest to get a key for the gate as the opening alongside wouldn't be wide enough for Sitka to get through.

Sitka and Pippin were very excited being able to run in the woods. We were winding our way along the track when suddenly a fox darted across the road in front of us and disappeared among the trees. Russet saw it and shot off after it, then Pippin shot off after Russet. As Sitka and I slowly walked on I heard crying behind me. It was Pippin who must have thought she had lost me again. Suddenly she saw me and raced up to me crying with excitement but there was no sign of Russet. I kept calling him and Sitka kept looking around for him as he always did when he couldn't see him. We continued on, as I would often think he was somewhere behind us then found him way ahead after all. He always knew which way we were heading.

Suddenly we heard a yell from among the trees ahead of us. There was a big ditch, then a clump of gorse bushes at the other side where the sound came from. I couldn't see anything so climbed down and over the ditch and then my eye caught sight of something moving in the bracken alongside the gorse bushes. Yes, it was Russet.

Pippin hadn't managed to get over the deep ditch, so was waiting watching me.

On again along the track when Russet suddenly darted forward. There ahead of us was the large fox staring at us. Away went Russet after it with Pippin following. Pippin was back very quickly and came up to me; not long afterwards Russet arrived back looking very subdued. Then I saw the same fox staring at us again and both terriers made no attempt to go after it this time.

We got through the woods back to Innellan then back to the farm we had been camping at near Dunoon. Next day we were to meet the pub landlord with his horse trailer. As it was a lovely fine morning, I decided we would go up the hill again and have a look at the view from the top right across the Firth of Clyde to Kilcreggan and Gourock.

The pub landlord arrived with the horse trailer early in the morning. I coaxed Sitka into it with carrots while both terriers watched wondering what was happening. Pippin kept her distance. She was far from sure it was safe to get too close.

Once Sitka was safely in the trailer, the three of us got into the landlord's pickup. Apart from the day I had picked her up as a seven-week-old puppy, Pippin hadn't been in a vehicle. She sat on my knee shivering at first but as we drove onto the ferry, she thought it all quite exciting. The ferry landed at the pier west of Gourock. The landlord dropped us off then drove back on the ferry to get back to Dunoon.

I had studied my map and decided we didn't need to go through the town, however I missed the turn off the main road at Ashton so we ended up going through the town after all. Eventually, we got to a single track, which took us right over the top by Loch Thom – but oh – the litter dumped alongside in the verges and dumped in ditches, in the woods and on the roadside. I wondered, did people come out to appreciate the countryside – no – they must come out to deliberately dump their rubbish without a thought for the countryside.

We had to tackle a very busy main road through Largs after camping in a beautiful spot near a stream near Whittlieburn. Then I was back to a single track road over to Dalry, with less litter as we got further away from the Gourock area. After Dalry, the countryside got very disappointing and unattractive and further on, the fields looked waterlogged and the stock grazing on them looked poor after all the wet weather. There were fields of wet cut grass waiting to be made into silage, but the fields were too wet to get machinery onto it. Occasionally, I would see a tractor pulling a bailer gathering up sodden wet grass and mud and think that it couldn't be good for whatever is supposed to eat it.

That evening we called at a farmhouse with converted stables and one field. "Yes, you are welcome to camp here. All our horses are in for the night so you can camp in the field." I looked at the field. Water was lying on the surface; the ground unable to absorb any more. When the couple who had welcomed us, saw the look on my face at the sight of the field, they led me to a hayshed and suggested I camp in there. Just as I was thinking Sitka would fit in there with us, a huge Alsatian dog came up towards us and then sat watching us. Pippin sat staring at it from her saddlebag and didn't move.

The couple left me putting my tent up in the hayshed by attaching the guy ropes to an old machine on one side then to the strings round bales of hay on the other side. Just as I was sorting out the saddlebags a voice called "Come and have supper with us!" I fed both terriers and left them in the tent then went across the yard to their house. Inside was the same huge Alsatian who kept eyeing me. "He's our watchdog" they explained "We leave him in the yard when we go to Glasgow each day; we have a fish shop there."

After supper, I was asked if I would like to use the bathroom and was directed to the staircase to go upstairs but the Alsatian blocked my way. "Occasionally he gets a bit above himself and won't let us go upstairs," they explained, "but otherwise he is OK." I didn't like the look on the beast's face but I pushed past him and he didn't object!

Next day, we managed to find a way skirting round Irvine. "This is a very deprived area" a fellow told me when I remarked on all the litter and mess lying about. "Does living in a deprived area mean you need to live in squalor?" I asked him, as the wind blew a pile of rubbish across the road in front of us.

As we continued on, I could hear the constant drone of traffic in the distance. It soon became one loud roar of racing vehicles and I realised there was a motorway ahead of us, but it was not marked on my map. As we got closer, I could see the road we were on went over and above the rushing traffic. Poor Sitka. He hated those flyovers over motorways. All those massive vehicles charging underneath him was very frightening.

They do show up the huge contrast between nature's pace of life and man's crazy way of living. You see sheep and cattle peacefully grazing or lying chewing their cud in fields alongside the roar of dashing vehicles. Birds sing cheerfully, yet are barely heard from the bushes or trees near the motorway banks where no one can possibly have time to notice them.

With all our travelling on roads, one of Sitka's hind shoes had snapped at the toe. It had come off so we stopped in a quiet spot and I tied him to a tree. Thankfully it wasn't raining, so I could get out the basic shoeing tools I had in the saddlebags and get out one of the spare shoes and replace it. Pippin thought it was all a great game grabbing the tools and running off with them. She had been sitting in the saddlebag a long time and was ready for some exercise, so I had to let her annoy me!

The countryside began to improve as we went on towards Kirkmichael then on to Dalrymple, but the weather didn't improve. We had a wild night on a farm with the little tent tucked in behind a silage trailer hoping

to have a bit of shelter, but the wind swept under the trailer and howled round the tent making it shudder violently. It was hard to sleep. I kept worrying that the tent pegs wouldn't hold, then the tent would sag and the driving rain would soak in. Twice I had to get up and drive the tent pegs back into the ground because they had come loose.

Next day was through the peaceful village of Straiton where we met a lady who wanted to interview me for the local newsletter. Then she went home to telephone a friend who lived three miles down the road to tell her I was on my way and she should meet me. We hadn't gone far when the friend turned up in her car and she insisted I went on to her place to stay.

When I got there, she said the dogs would have to stay in the shed as she had a German pointer in the house and he wouldn't approve of the dogs coming into the house. I managed to persuade her to let me camp in the field where she let me graze Sitka, so that I didn't have to desert my two terriers and leave them in a shed overnight.

Once I had fed the dogs and they had settled on my sleeping bag, I accepted the invitation to supper in the house and heard all about the host's days of running a riding school in Epsom and how she started up the riding school licencing scheme.

For the first time during this trip, I woke up to find frost on the tent and no sound of rain. Maybe we were going to have some fine sunny days as often happens after frosty nights. Sure enough, the sun did come out and it was a beautiful day as we headed towards Newton Stewart.

As we were passing a farm a man came running towards me calling as if he knew me. "Please come in and have a cup of coffee with me," he insisted. He seemed desperate for company so I tied up Sitka and let the terriers out of their saddlebags and followed him into the farmhouse, then heard all about his wife lying dying in hospital of cancer and how he was having great difficulty coping with the farm work and seeing to his own needs as well as visiting the hospital each day. Then he told me of all the different people he had persuaded to come into his house for coffee or tea over the summer – Australians, Germans, Americans as well as English and Scottish. It was difficult to get on my way again. I think he would have gone on talking all day and got no farm work done at all.

We were heading towards Creetown and it was going to be impossible to avoid several miles of that terrible main road, the A75, with all its Irish traffic heading to and from the ferry at Stranraer. As it was a Sunday, I hoped it would be quieter with a little less heavy traffic, so we hadn't to waste any more time to be sure of getting there before dusk. We only just made it. The traffic was awful but I could only assume it was better than if it were a week day. We turned off the main road just as it got dusk, and found a farm to camp at. I noticed a very strong smell of billy goats.

Once the tent was up and Sitka safely grazing, the three of us got into the tent. The smell of billy goats got stronger. It was Russet. He stank of billy goat, but when and where had he rolled and picked up that awful pong?

From Creetown we went over the hill road then down a wet muddy track to Gatehouse of Fleet where we were caught by a reporter who was all excited about seeing two terriers in saddlebags on a pack pony. He asked a lot of questions then proceeded to take a lot of photographs. All the time Pippin was wriggling to get out of her saddlebag, but she didn't find it so easy now she had grown quite a bit over our weeks away. She could no longer slip out of the safety strap that held her in place.

In spite of having a few fine days and frosty nights all my things were damp. The days were much shorter now that we were in October and condensation is always a problem when the weather gets colder. The tent can be as wet with condensation as it can be with rain, and when putting a tent up on a frosty night all the wet freezes into a layer of ice. It can be so stiff with a layer of ice on a frosty morning it is impossible to wrap up.

It was another beautiful day as we went up by Lauriston and stopped by some trees in brilliant sunshine. I got the spare rope and made a clothes line and hung all the camping gear on it to dry out. Then we all made the most of the sun and lay on the heather. Once the waterproof sheet that I used to cover all the packs plus terriers in their saddlebags on Sitka, was dry, I laid it out on the ground and got out the repair kit to stick patches on all the holes. They were only tiny pricks, usually from thorns on bushes we couldn't avoid when diving into verges at the side of the road to get out of the way of speeding vehicles, but even a tiny pin prick can let enough heavy rain through to wet what is underneath.

After the repairing session, I got some dry bracken and a few sticks then got a fire going and heated up some water from the stream near by in my camping pan and had a good wash.

It was a beautiful evening, so still and peaceful. The sun had gone down behind the hills leaving a picturesque display of colours in the sky. A friendly farmer had let us camp in a field near the farm with a magnificent view of all the hills around us.

There was a flock of sheep grazing at the far end of the field. I unloaded all the packs off Sitka then tied up Pippin by her lead to the fence.

I saw the sheep down the field raise their heads. They had seen Sitka grazing and were staring at him. Next, I was aware of a large Suffolk tup walking determinedly toward the tent with all his women coming behind him. His eyes were fixed on his target – he was going to charge at the tent. I ran towards him to chase him off but he only stood his ground, stamped his feet, and looked as if he was going to charge at me. Russet was sitting surveying the situation while Pippin was straining at the end of her lead tied to the fence. The more I shooed, the more excited she became.

Suddenly he made a charge and I grabbed the ground sheet I was going to put under the tent and ran towards him flapping it violently, then Russet leapt to my assistance. Between us we managed to chase him off as high-pitched cries of excitement came from Pippin who was desperate to join in the fun.

The whole flock fled to the far end of the field again but it wasn't long before he was back again. This time he kept a distance yet keeping an eye on us all the time. I just hoped he wouldn't get a sudden bout of courage during the night and have another go at the tent!

Next day took us to Castle Douglas. It was as chaotic as Hexham is on a busy market day. Crowds of people and traffic cluttered the place so we fled quickly and gave up any idea of stopping for provisions.

That night, we got to Brow Hill near Dalbeattie – Sitka's birth place where I first saw him as a very young foal. He was playing around his mother who was grazing peacefully at the top of the field next to Sitka Spruce trees. That was nearly twenty years ago and this was his sixteenth autumn trip as a pack pony.

Catherine was waiting for us by her bungalow as I unloaded everything off Sitka and put my camping gear in her garage. Both terriers ran towards her as she called out "The kettle is on ready to make a cup of tea!" She had met Russet many times over the years but not Pippin. Russet remembered that there are masses of rabbits all around the place and soon shot off to chase them but Pippin was too busy wriggling with excitement as Catherine greeted her.

We planned to stay a few days with Catherine and let Sitka have a well-earned rest. Sitting in her living room both terriers decided there was plenty room for them both on my knee which was a bit awkward yet they both slept that first day as they were both really tired.

The next day, we were having a cup of tea sitting watching the view out of the large window facing south over Catherine's garden and down towards the coast and the hills beyond. The rabbits weren't used to any dogs about and hadn't any fear of anything. They ran about and grazed on Catherine's lawn right below the window. Both terriers soon realised if they sat on my knee they could see out of the window and watch the rabbits, then with sudden yelps of excitement leap off my knee, dash to the French window to be let out to chase them. Then once all were chased away, they wanted to be let back in again to get onto my knee and watch and wait until more rabbits dared to return. Fortunately, after a day or two, the rabbits got wise to what it was like to have dogs about and got far more cautious about coming into the garden. At first, we found it amusing, but after a while it got ridiculous because neither Russet nor Pippin would settle down on my knee; then Russet would get annoyed with Pippin and they started quarrelling over getting the best position on my knee to be able to see the out of the window and wait for a rabbit to come into view.

It was my third day at Brow Hill and now time to do the last lap home. Days were getting very short now as it was getting to the end of October. That last evening, I was getting all my things collected together ready to get a good start in the morning. Both terriers had got all the local rabbits well chased and very cautious about daring to come into the garden. They watched me packing my things into the saddlebags. Russet knew well we were about to be on our way again and followed me about keeping an eye on me. Pippin watched Russet and sensed something was going to happen too so followed him about keeping an eye on him all the time.

"The water's hot for your last bath before you go," Catherine called out.

With two terriers following me, I went into the bathroom. Russet soon thought that watching me having a bath was a bit boring, so sat on the bathmat with his head hanging while Pippin couldn't understand what I was doing so leapt up and down trying to join me in the bath.

It was back to wet weather as we left Catherine's. My boots were so worn they were not only letting in water but gravel and loose stones were also coming in the soles. We had to go through Dumfries. To avoid the town would have been a long way round. It was getting too late to be adding on extra miles. I planned to try to get some new boots in the town.

Roads through the town were awfully busy. There is such a lot of traffic passing through and only two bridges over the River Nith, which flows from north to south through the centre of the town. We got over the St Michael's bridge but I could feel Sitka getting more and more anxious about all the heavy traffic roaring past him. We turned right once over the bridge and I tied him up on The Sands with both terriers in their saddlebags, then went in search of a shop selling boots.

I could hear anxious neighing from Sitka. He didn't want to be left with traffic roaring all around – he was beginning to panic so I went back to him and stood with him for a while, then tried again to find some boots ignoring his yells and hoping he would still be there when I got back!

Feeling a bit awkward with the sudden change of having new boots on my feet I ran back towards The Sands. Trying to cross the road, which was so busy, I had to wait and wait until there was an opportunity to make a run for it. Sitka and Pippin were both yelling with excitement as I returned, relieved to see all three were still there. I untied Sitka and was dragged away; so determined was he to get out of the town as quickly as possible.

We were soon out of the town and going along the coast road past Bankend and towards Ruthwell to camp on the coast by the Solway Firth when what must have been thousands of barnacle geese flew over us - a magnificent sight, and what a noise they made.

The next day we went on by Cannonbie and through to Newcastleton then back into Kielder Forest the following day in yet more rain, on to Tarset, then home.

Home to Pippin was the tent after seven weeks away; she had forgotten what her short life was like before. Sitka soon adapted back to his role as a riding school pony carrying a variety of children learning how to ride. His days of carrying older children were over and he now carried lightweight beginners only.

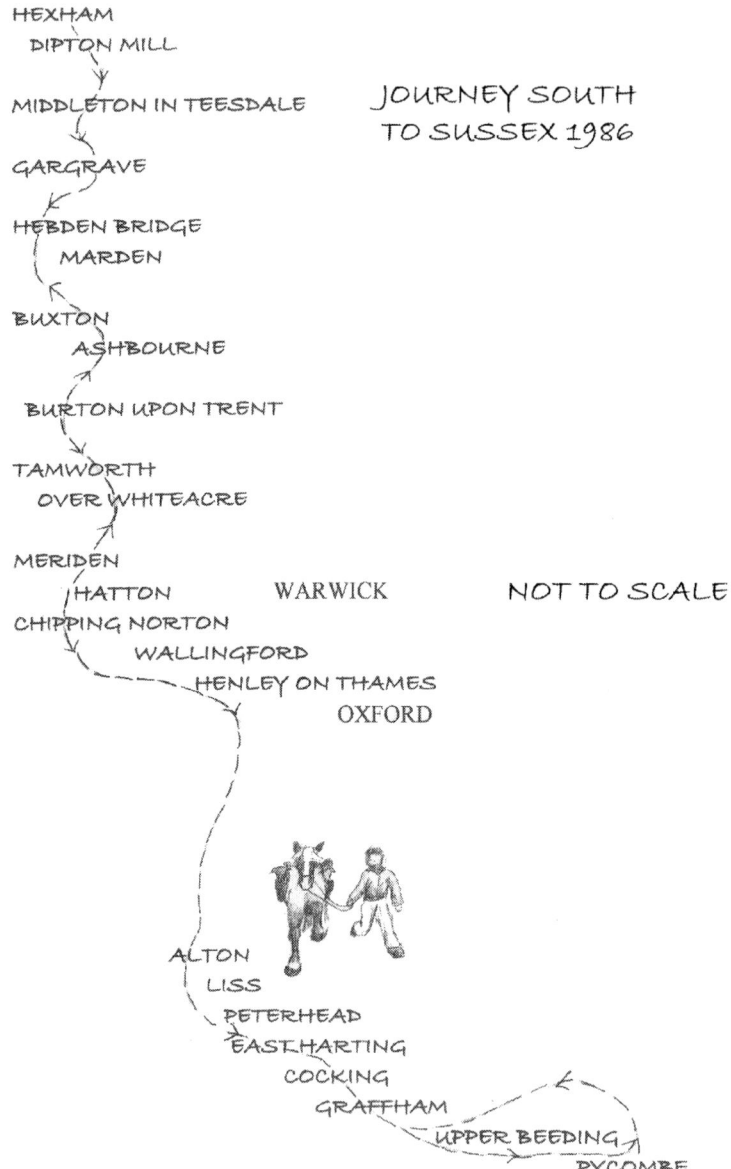

HEXHAM
DIPTON MILL
MIDDLETON IN TEESDALE
GARGRAVE
HEBDEN BRIDGE
MARDEN
BUXTON
ASHBOURNE
BURTON UPON TRENT
TAMWORTH
OVER WHITEACRE
MERIDEN
HATTON   WARWICK
CHIPPING NORTON
    WALLINGFORD
       HENLEY ON THAMES
          OXFORD

ALTON
LISS
PETERHEAD
EASTHARTING
COCKING
GRAFFHAM
    UPPER BEEDING
       PYCOMBE

JOURNEY SOUTH
TO SUSSEX 1986

NOT TO SCALE

2

JOURNEY SOUTH TO SUSSEX
WITH SITKA, RUSSET & PIPPIN

September 1986

Pippin was now over a year old and fully grown but still a lot smaller than Russet. The school summer holidays were just about over. Sitka's horrid cancerous growth was no worse and I had managed to stop Russet going off hunting rabbits down the bank so I didn't lose him again down a burrow.

We were all four of us ready to set off on our annual autumn journey. Both terriers had seen me packing the saddlebags, so were keeping a watchful eye on me. Sitka knew the signs of what was about to happen when all the other ponies had been turned out to graze and he was the only one left in the stable.

After several invitations from friends I had got to know through previous journeys south, I decided to trek down to Sussex again. If it hadn't been for the excellent bridleway system in parts of the south, especially in Sussex, I wouldn't have been so tempted to head in that direction. To be able to travel for miles right through the heart of the countryside off roads away from traffic has a fascination and a thrill about it. The overall beauty of Scotland's countryside surpasses all I have seen but before the introduction of their new Countryside Code, the lack of rights of way to travel with a horse so having to trudge along so many roads with speeding traffic, spoiled it. Whichever way I go, north or south, there are the horrible bits to get through; that busy area between Edinburgh and

Glasgow if going north and that midland area with lack of bridleways if going south.

It was 6.30 on a Monday morning when we set off up through Slaley Forest then over to Blanchland moors to Bay Bridge. Both terriers were able to run along beside Sitka as I led the old chap who was getting very slow in his old age. That gave the two terriers plenty of time to go rabbiting then catch up. That evening we camped up above Westgate in Teesdale, then climbed up over Swinhope and over to Middleton-in-Teesdale next morning. Sitka had put on extra weight over the summer in spite of me trying to keep him on a diet. He huffed and puffed up the hills and kept stopping to rest. At first, he had me worried that he was ailing, but as the journey progressed and he lost a bit of weight, the huffing and puffing got less and less and the stops for a rest got shorter.

In areas where there is a poor rabbit population, Russet and Pippin would run on ahead of us. Russet had a habit of running back towards me barking as if to say hurry up - you're too slow! Pippin soon found this a good game so the two of them, after running on ahead, would stop, turn around, and watch Sitka and me plodding slowly up a steep hill then race back towards us barking.

Fortunately, in most areas where they could run freely and not be in their saddlebags, there were plenty of rabbits and they often ended up chasing us to catch up.

Both Sitka and Russet had done the route south many times over the years, and both knew our regular stopping places. We had got to one of those regular stopping places after travelling through the Yorkshire Dales and Sitka automatically turned and pulled me into the farm entrance. It was understood that if there was nobody at the farmhouse I could go into the field and pitch my tent so I let both terriers down out of their saddlebags and Russet ran off around the corner and started barking at the back door of the house. Pippin looked at me then cocked her ear to listen to Russet. I heard the door open and a voice called out "Is that you

Russet?" Pippin then shot off to see where Russet was and who was talking to him. "Who is this you have with you, Russet?" By the time Sitka and I got round the corner, both terriers were in the house getting a biscuit each. "Get your tent up in the usual place Jane, then come in and join us!"

The tent up and Sitka safely grazing, I walked round to the farmhouse and joined Russet and Pippin who were now in the living room by the fire. At the end of the living room was a bed with a frail figure in it. It was three years since we had last called at the farm, and thirteen years since we first camped there. The well-built hard-working fellow I met those thirteen years ago was now a pale emaciated man who had deteriorated so much since I last saw him that I could hardly recognise him. He could only just hold the glass of whisky he so depended on and from the pile of cigarette ends in the ashtrays on his bedside table, cigarettes were also still a necessity in his failing life.

Back in the tent I thought how sad that the emaciated figure I saw lying on that bed looked like someone from a famine-stricken country, rather than from a 'land of plenty;' a successful respected farmer living in a beautiful area of the countryside - may be plenty was not enough.

It was only mid September but I woke up to a layer of frost on the tent. Both terriers felt like me – reluctant to move. I was warm in my sleeping bag with two warm bodies lying by my feet keeping my toes warm. By the time we did move there was a slight glimmer of sun peering over the horizon. If we got ourselves on the move we could stop at lunchtime and get defrosted in the sun. I told the dogs but they were still reluctant to move! I pushed them out of the tent and wrapped it all up stuffing everything into the saddlebags. By the time we did get away the sun was well out so Russet and Pippin's enthusiasm was warmed up.

By lunch time it was a really beautiful day. We stopped by a gate in a wall for our lunch and I hung all the camping things out to defrost. A farmer was away across a field nearby collecting his sheep with a collie dog. How the collie dog knew we were there I don't know. I doubted it could have seen us. He was a very long way away and was very busy obeying its master's instructions. Suddenly he appeared right next to us. I grabbed Pippin as the wretched thing cocked his leg and had a wee all over the tent hanging on the wall. Then he dashed off and was back with his master rounding up sheep. I ended up having to wash the tent in a nearby stream so that it was wetter than it was from the melting frost before I hung it up.

We were running short of milk. I had used it all in my coffee and the essential pan of porridge each day. It had to be coffee without milk that lunch time and the dogs were most put out not getting their drop of milk after sharing my bread and cheese.

That afternoon a van stopped in the side of a narrow road to let us past. I noticed the back of the van was full of bottled milk. "Could I buy some milk from you?" I asked.

"Yes, dear!" and he got out of his van. "Which do you want? Red top, silver top or green top?"

Being used to milking my own cow I replied, "I just want milk!"

"You mean this stuff with cream on?" he asked.

"Yes!" Then he proceeded to tell me how he couldn't understand the health fad that had gripped most of his customers "Most ask for skimmed milk because it is better for them and there they are standing with a fag in their mouths. I'm sure it's more likely to kill them than the cream!" Then "t'others," he went on to tell me, "have skimmed milk all week but at weekends order a large carton of cream as a special treat!"

As we got further south, I met a lady waving frantically at me so I stopped and she caught me up. "I've been trying to contact you as I've got a friend who does long distance endurance riding," she explained. "She set off from south of Hexham early in September to try and follow the Pennine Way and I know you came down through that area and might have been able to give her some advice. It's probably a bit late now as I think she will nearly be finished."

It turned out that she had started her journey the same time as I had started and here we were several miles ahead at our slow pace. It certainly wasn't our speed that kept us ahead. We were only going at walking pace. Endurance riders trot and canter but I doubted they travelled the long hours that we did each day. We were now heading for Buxton to stay with my sister at Harper Hill just outside the town for a few days. On the way, I was to visit a lovely old lady who always asked me in for a cup of tea and liked to chat and feed Russet with biscuits.

I tied Sitka up to the nearest tree on the roadside just outside her house as all she had was a little patch of lawn between her house and the road – hardly enough to stand a pony on and if I had tried to fit him into the space, I felt sure she wouldn't want horses' hooves ploughing up her grass. It was only a narrow road, but with Sitka tied to the tree, there was still plenty of space for cars to pass behind him. He had been tied up in that same spot over the years so stood quietly as Pippin and I joined Russet who was already in the house being fed biscuits.

Suddenly there was a loud knock on the door and a man's voice shouted "There's a loose horse galloping down the road!" I opened the door and there was a huge double-decker bus full of passengers and the frantic driver trying to explain to me that the horse tied to the tree had reared up and snapped his rope then shot off ahead of the bus and every time he tried to drive on it bolted ahead of him.

I ran down the road and eventually caught up with Sitka and managed to get him into an opening off the road as the bus driver drove past us with a wave of relief, or thank you, or maybe both; his passengers staring out of the windows as if they didn't really believe what they had just seen.

Back at the house Russet and Pippin gave me a great welcome. I think they thought Sitka and I had gone off without them.

"No, you're alright, that big bus only comes once a week to collect people round about who want to go shopping. You'll be alright tying Sitka back on that tree," I was told, but he wasn't happy about the idea so we continued on after a quick cup of tea and yet more biscuits for the dogs.

We stayed at Harper Hill for a few days then continued on south joining the Tissington Trail to Ashbourne: the old Buxton Railway track to Ashbourne which is now a cycle, riders' and walkers' route ideal for two terriers to be free to run and look for rabbits in the banks at the side of the tracks.

Then we camped at Yeaveley where many years ago I met John and Maureen who had seen me passing by and recognised Sitka as a Haflinger. Back then they had a Haflinger mare, so were interested to know where I had got Sitka from. They offered me a lovely spot to camp on their land which is now a regular camping spot on all our journeys south.

There are some very picturesque villages in the south once through the Tamworth Area. A notice in one village amused me. It was by their public toilets - PUBLIC TOILETS, NOT SUITABLE FOR VEHICLES - I assumed it was there to tell folk there were public toilets but not really room to park their vehicles!

It was always noticeable how much milder the weather is when one gets further south. It had been pretty cold all the way south so far but the temperature rose after we left Buxton. That meant we had the familiar camping visitors; spiders dangling on the end of their web ropes after I lit my camping gas stove. I never noticed them climbing up there, but am very aware of them trying to escape the heat because they often dangle on their rope webs and are inclined to drop into the pan of porridge on the stove. Slugs get less sluggish as the weather gets warmer especially when conditions are warm and damp. I can never understand why they must climb up inside the tent. There is nothing worse than a slug dropping inside the pan of porridge! Pulling them off the tent isn't pleasant either. They leave that awful sticky slime on the fingers which doesn't easily wash off.

We met a farmer coming towards us as we were getting down into Warwickshire. He was carrying a bucket. Sitka thought he had feed for him in the bucket and tried to pull me towards it. "I'm not sure you would like this," the man said to Sitka as he held out his hand with some of the contents of the bucket on it. "It is for my goats, I'm just off to feed them." Sitka soon showed him that he fully approved of what was in his hands and would gladly eat what was in the bucket as well if he could. I had to firmly drag him away as the farmer explained he was off to milk his goats and he used the milk to feed his calves and for himself although he had a dairy farm.

He went on to tell me how he kept his goats on some of the land that had no artificial fertiliser put on it and were fed organically home grown corn mixture but his cows had to be fed on bought in non-organic daily feed and grazed on land which he spread with artificial fertiliser because he couldn't afford to be totally organic. "So, I don't drink the cow's milk, only the goat's milk," he said, then asked me if I would like to camp on his farm.

Later, once the tent was up, he asked me in for supper and told me about his concerns about all the chemical fertiliser used on farms these days and also the concern he had over all the ingredients that are put into animal feeds. His father had kept bullocks in a yard on very deep straw all winter to make sure he had plenty of manure to spread on his land in the spring. What really surprised me when he talked about his land management, was that he had no qualms about spraying several acres of his land with weed killer to kill all the grass before ploughing it.

My maps were getting out of date since our first trips south thirteen years ago. We had already found a new motorway right across our route – the M42. Our usual route had been closed off. We ended up having to go along the busy A5 for a mile or so. Sitka was terrified of the traffic speeding past him. Both terriers were fastened into their saddlebags. Every time a big vehicle went past, Sitka jumped forward and the jerking movement made his mane bounce up. Pippin was leaning out of the saddlebag trying to catch bits of bobbing mare and tugging at it.

Some miles on we came to a dual carriageway. There was so much traffic it was impossible to find a pause long enough to get over both carriageways in one go. After waiting and waiting and still more waiting I decide to make a dash for it over the first carriageway then hope there would soon be a pause long enough to get over the second carriageway.

There was a brief moment when we were stuck in between both carriageways with traffic flying past in front of us and behind us, before we could make a dash and get across the far carriageway to join the old road which had been sliced through by the new road.

Then, oh horror, the road had been fenced across with only a narrow pedestrian gate in the middle not really wide enough to get a pack pony through. I wasn't going back over that dual carriageway. The saddlebags would have to come off then hopefully Sitka could squeeze through the narrow gate. The terriers had to come out of the saddlebags and be tied to the fence. With the saddle packs off Sitka, he just managed to squeeze though the gateway. I then hoisted the packs back onto him and lifted both terriers into their bags.

We hadn't gone far when we came to another fence across the road with a narrow wicket gate no wider than the one we had already come through. Not only that, but another main road not marked on my map was on the other side of the gate. Where was the old road we wanted to be on? I tied Sitka to the fence and went through the wicket gate to see how we could avoid having to go down the main road which had sliced through the road we wanted. Yes, there it was just a few yards further down the main road and with no fence across it. So, off with the saddlebags once more to get Sitka through the narrow gate. We were awfully close to the flying traffic on the main road. There wasn't much room to tie Sitka up on the outside of the fence while putting the saddlebags back onto him. He was getting more and more upset as huge vehicles roared past him with that awful swish of air and blast of exhaust fumes. Even Russet and Pippin kept ducking as the vast vehicles passed so near to where they were tied to the fence.

Between swearing and cursing, I did manage to think how grateful I was that it wasn't raining so that everything didn't get wet. Sitka had got himself so worked up over having to be tied up so near the speeding traffic I had great difficulty controlling him down the few yards on the main road to join the old road again. He was ready to bolt off if I let go of the rein. He was nearly dragging me along. Then we had to stop and wait for a pause in the traffic long enough to cross the road. At least it wasn't a dual carriageway this time.

I began to think "Never again am I venturing south with all its new roads slicing through the countryside and all its volume of traffic going at such a speed."

Once on the old road, we began to relax. We stopped at a small village shop and I went in to get provisions and got a very warm welcome. They remembered me from four years ago. I went back to put the provisions in the saddlebags and the woman from the shop ran after me with a large bag of carrots for Sitka.

Thoughts of this being our last trip south were fading as we continued along quiet roads and lanes. Then – what was that ahead of us? I could hear a loud engine. It sounded like a large vehicle and we were on a very narrow road. Where could I get out of the way before it got here? Then I saw it was a hedge-cutter in the field ahead., not on the road. There were bits of hedge-cuttings flying across the road. We stopped, hoping the driver would see us and stop to let us past. Yes, he must have seen us because the engine stopped, so we continued on. We were just about level with him when it suddenly started up again. He hadn't seen us, it was just a coincidence that he had stopped when he did. This time I couldn't hold Sitka and he shot forward quickly. Fortunately, both dogs were out of their saddlebags, but we all got an awful fright as we were showered with hedge cuttings.

Sitka stopped and waited for us as soon as he got far enough away from the sudden roar of the tractor starting up and showering hedge cuttings.

On down the road and Pippin was trailing behind us. She was limping, what was the matter? We stopped to wait for her. She was holding her front paw and looking very sad and in pain. I lifted her up and looked at her paw. A huge thorn had got itself stuck in one of the pads of her foot.

I pulled it out then put her down again – she then ran to catch up with Russet and forgot about it.

Now I was cursing modern farm machinery and my thoughts went back to when we had a local hedge cutter; a lovely old chap who spent his days cutting hedges by hand and took great pride in his work. He knew every bird and animal that lived in those hedgerows and would talk to them or would be whistling cheerfully as he worked. I suppose these days such a job may be considered boring or underpaid.

We were getting into Oxfordshire and going to a farm where Sitka, Russet and I had camped several times on previous trips south. The weather was beautiful and the bridleways good. We were able to go miles across country away from the traffic. Both Russet and Pippin were able to run and chase rabbits, but it wasn't long before Pippin found a new sport – putting up pheasants and leaping in the air as they took off to try and catch them before they flew away. Russet watched them for a while then decided it was far too energetic a game so put his nose down to search for the scent of a rabbit. Unfortunately, we hadn't gone far when I had to put a stop to it.

We met a man walking beside us. I assumed he was a game keeper. He wasn't at all pleased to have his pheasants chased and told me I had to stop my dog from disturbing his birds.

That night we camped in the overgrown garden of a farm cottage. The farmer had two students living in the cottage while they were working for him. The lawn was like a hayfield so Sitka soon had his head down mowing it. Later the students arrived looking soiled and exhausted. They had been ploughing from 7:30 am until 9:30 pm every day for two weeks and had another 600 acres to plough before they left to go back to agricultural college.

All the way through Oxfordshire into Berkshire there were acres and acres of unfenced land all ploughed for growing corn. The land looked heavy and the soil 'dead' as if it lacked humus. It was so compacted down by all the heavy machinery used on it. I noticed some tractors on the very heavy looking land had double back wheels to give it the extra grip needed to get the plough through the compacted soil.

Into Hook Norton to call on Mrs Windier who lived in a lovely little thatched cottage in the village. Russet, Sitka and I had camped on an area of grass outside her cottage twice on previous trips south. Sadly, this time she wasn't in, and it was getting late. Do I just camp there and hope she won't mind or do I go on? I decided to carry on. A few miles further on and who should stop in her car but Mrs Windier. "Are you going to come back and camp at my cottage?" It goes against the grain to go back so I said, "I'll go on and come back to see you on my way home again." We went on, but where was I going to camp? It began to get dark and I needed to get off the road. Then I saw a lovely spot in a gateway between trees. "We'll go in there for the night." Sitka thought it was well past time to stop, so we went in and settled for the night but I kept feeling guilty camping on someone's land without asking permission first. Next morning, we made an early start before anyone saw us!

We were heading for Henley-on-Thames to see an old school friend who lived there. There was no way we could avoid busy roads to get there. The traffic was awful particularly at commuter times when drivers are in such a hurry. After a couple of nights there with Sitka tethered on her large lawn, we continued to Pangbourne then were thankful to get back onto bridleways. Most of the farms appeared to have no livestock, just acres of unfenced land with corn growing on it. It was difficult sometimes to find a farm with a grass area we could camp on. Late one evening I asked at a farm and the farmer suggested I go to a bit of woodland he had down the lane where there was an area of grass between the trees. We were welcome to camp there.

Suddenly, in the middle of the night, I heard the roar of a motorbike engine then it stopped near us and all went very quiet, so I went back to sleep again. It was still dark when Russet sat up and barked. Had he heard someone? I heard sounds as if Sitka was struggling. Had he got tangled up in his tether rope? I'd better go and see. By the time I got my glasses and boots on, both terriers had shot out of the tent barking. Then there was the roar of a motorbike starting up and away it went. With my head torch on. I got out of the tent and a pathetic whinnying came from Sitka. I shone my torch where the sound came from and there he was lying on the ground with his tether rope wound round his legs so that he was unable to move at all.

It took me a while to get the rope from around his legs, it had got so tight with him trying to get up. "How long have you been wound up like that?" It must have been a while because at first he couldn't get up after I got the rope free. Then when I managed to persuade him to get onto his feet he seemed very unsteady for a while. What had happened? Had someone deliberately wound the rope around his legs or had he been so frightened and spun round a few times and got the rope caught on his legs? The farmer had told me that there was an awful lot of bother with poachers in the area. Because so many of the fields are unfenced and ploughed over to grow acres and acres of corn, poachers can drive over the land, let their lurchers free to catch deer or hares and follow them in their vehicles.

Perhaps that motorbike had been a poacher, but I would never know. It just gave an air of fear of who could be around and up to no good.

I joined the South Downs Way at East Harting. It is a lovely route along the Sussex South Downs. Before leaving I had written to the pub at Pyecombe to see if they knew anyone who could let me camp on their land for a few days so I could get a bus into Brighton to visit an old friend who had retired near the coast. I had looked at the map and chosen Pyecombe because it was on the main road to Brighton and felt sure there would be a bus service into town. The owner of the pub wrote back to say yes, they had a customer who had a paddock beside his house at Pyecombe and I was welcome to use it.

I had been through Pyecombe with Sitka and Russet in 1980 and again in 1982 when we came south to go along the South Down Way and the number of vehicles on the road seemed bad then. Now it was four years later. When we got to where the route crosses over the dual carriageway at Pyecombe, the number of vehicles were frightening. I had both terriers on their leads, thinking we only had to cross the road then they could run free again; it wasn't worth putting them in their saddlebags again. We ended up getting stuck in the middle of the dual carriageway with traffic racing past in front of us and charging past behind us. Sitka began to get nervous and to panic. I could feel I was going to lose control of him and was beginning to panic myself.

Suddenly, the lady from the saddlery shop over the road saw what was happening and came out frantically waving her arms in the air and bravely stepped into the road and stopped all the traffic. It was amazing how she managed to get all those vehicles to skid to a halt. No one got damaged and we got across safely.

I found the house of the owner of the paddock and explained who I was. "I'm afraid the riding school horses in the field next door to my paddock have knocked the fence down and are all in the paddock. You'd be better camping in my garden," he said, then took me to his garden behind his house. There was a rough area by some trees by the fence at the top where I could see a large number of ponies and horses grazing in what looked like his paddock. "Will that do?" he asked, pointing to the rough area. There wasn't much for Sitka to eat, but there was room to put the tent up and to have Sitka tethered up with enough grazing for one night.

Next day I had arranged to go on the bus to Brighton, but the forecast was rain. I couldn't leave the terriers in the tent all day, so rigged up a shelter for them with an old door I found lying by the fence and propped it up on some large rocks and mounds of earth as a shelter.

When I got back, Pippin was howling with excitement, but Russet was fast asleep. I untied Sitka and led him up the track, which was back on the South Downs Way and tethered him on a good grassy area. I then took two excited terriers for a walk leaving Sitka to eat as much grass as he could before the four of us returned to our garden camping spot.

It was getting late in the year; we had to go all the way back north to Northumberland. Another week and it would be November so I decided we had better not go any further along the South Downs, but make our way homeward. Days were getting very short so now we had to stop earlier before it got dark. We had been invited to stay a night in Graffham with a lovely lady I had met on previous trips who lived in a luxury log 'cabin'. Then we were to stay with a friend who had moved from Hexham and now lived in Liss.

The weather had turned very cold and frosty. One morning I couldn't get out of the tent because the zip had frozen. The three of us decided it was too cold to go out anyway so went back to sleep again. By the time we woke up it had thawed a bit as the sun came out, so all three of us shot out of the tent desperate for a pee.

By the time we got up to Hook Norton it was November. Mrs Windier was there in her lovely little thatched cottage. Sitka grazed on her grassed area by the cottage but the dogs and I slept on the bed settee in the cottage. She insisted we stay inside as it was so cold outside. Russet and Pippin fully agreed that we were better off inside! I had to drag two reluctant dogs out for their evening pee and to see if Sitka was alright.

When we arrived in Warwickshire we went back to the farm we had camped at on our way south. "You had better camp down there," I was told "you will get some shelter from that shed because there's gales forecast tonight."

I got the tent pitched then fed both terriers and left them in the tent as I had been invited into the farmhouse for something to eat. It was so dark when I came out that I only just found the tent again. All three of us settled in for the night. I could hear Sitka grazing nearby. It was quiet and we fell asleep.

I remember waking sometime later and hearing rain on the tent. It can feel nice and cosy in the tent in a dry and warm sleeping bag when it rains outside. I drifted off to sleep again. There was something wet by my head. It was water – lots of water! More and more water kept pouring into the tent. I leapt up. The rain was beating down but as well as hearing rain I could also hear fast flowing water. It took me a while to realise what was happening. The large shed had a drainpipe which should have led the water off the roof running down into a drain, but it was broken so all the water was cascading out of the broken pipe and straight on us.

There was nothing for it but to evacuate the tent, grab all I could and run into the shed and dump all the things inside.; it took several journeys to collect all that had been in the tent. I also had to persuade two reluctant dogs out into the rain to join me in the shed. There was just enough room among the machinery to spread out empty feed sacks from a pile in one end of the shed; I then put the sleeping bag on the top so that the three of us were not lying on the hard concrete floor.

Our next stop was on the farm where the farmer had farmed with his father for many years. When his father died he was left on his own to run the farm. The weather was awful. Cold wet and windy. "That barn is empty. You'll be better in there than camping," he said. I agreed and he helped me carry all the packs into the cow shed which had a thick bed of wood shavings on the floor. It was lovely and springy to lie on but with all that wet in the tent the previous night, the wood shavings stuck to all the wet things. The dog's feet were wet so spread wood shavings all over my sleeping bag.

"Come and have something to eat with me." I could see if I didn't go in the house with him he would have stood there talking and talking so I left the two dogs lying on my sleeping bag and went into the house with him. It was very much a bachelor house. "I get readymade meals and put them in the freezer as I'm no cook and it saves me a lot of bother."

It certainly was a quickly prepared meal but the plastic plate kept sliding about when I was trying to eat. He kept repeating interesting quotes he remembered his father telling him. I can only remember one now: "If you have two men working for you, a bad one and a good one, you can end up with two bad ones and never two good ones."

The next evening we met a farmer who said he had been watching us slogging up the hill towards his farm as he was mending his fence on the roadside. Then he offered me a field to camp in for the night.

I hadn't realised that it was November 5th and as I was putting the tent up there was a loud bang, then another, and another. Fireworks! Sitka stood looking horrified and frightened while Russet and Pippin sat shaking. Each time there was a long pause they began to relax then suddenly more bangs and they froze in horror. By the time I got the tent up and my things sorted inside it the loud bangs had stopped. Sitka began to graze again, then both terriers made a dash for the tent and dived into my sleeping bag.

We were in Derbyshire now and with the days getting shorter it wasn't always possible to get to the camp spots we'd used on the way south. They were too far apart for me to cover the mileage before it got dark.

"Yes, you are welcome to camp here," one farmer said. "You can go in the bull's field over there!"

"Is the bull in the field? "I asked him.

"Yes, but he'll do you no harm. He's very quiet," he replied.

"Can I put my pony in with the bull but pitch my tent on the grass on this side of the wall, by the gate?"

"Yes, if you prefer to," he said, then left us. I put Sitka through the gate into the bull's field but could see no bull. Next morning, I went to call Sitka. He came trotting towards me followed by the bull. Even Pippin wasn't too sure about that bull. He looked too big to argue with. Fortunately, he didn't attempt to follow Sitka as I led him out of the field through the gate. He stood watching me as if I had taken away his new friend.

With having two terriers, one egged the other one on; it was more exciting having a companion to hunt and chase rabbits with. Pippin was young and very fit but Russet was ten years older and finding he was tiring long before Pippin even showed signs of wanting to slow down. One day Russet looked at me as Pippin was chasing about looking for rabbits. I could see he had had enough, so picked him up and put him in his saddlebag. He sank into it with a look of relief on his face, then sat there watching Pippin.

We were on a bridleway. I could hear a tractor engine but thought nothing of it as it seemed to be in the distance, across some fields. Then suddenly it appeared through an open gateway onto the track we were on. Like double decker buses, Sitka hates tractors with a bucket up in the air in front of it. In a flash, he spun round and was off in full flight up the track with Russet bobbing about in his saddlebag. There was no chance of me holding on to him. All I could do was hope the packs didn't slip sideways then end up underneath Sitka and that Russet would not be chucked out of his saddlebag. Pippin thought the whole procedure was great fun and raced after Sitka yapping with excitement.

I ran after them but soon ran out of puff. There was no chance of me running to catch them up. I just hoped Sitka would eventually stop - which he did - and I did catch up. Russet seemed quite unconcerned and sat in his saddlebag looking at Pippin who danced up and down showing us she wanted to continue the fun.

Fortunately, the tractor was just crossing over the bridleway into a gateway opposite the one he had come through. The driver did wait to see if I managed to take control of the situation. When I turned round and waved to him, he drove on and we continued onwards – at a walking pace!

Later that day, we stopped to picnic. Russet decided he would join Pippin chasing rabbits but as there were so many rabbits about, and they both forgot to share my bread and cheese lunch. I had my mug of coffee in my hands when suddenly a rabbit shot round behind me and disappeared down a hole under a tree stump. A few seconds later the two terriers came racing past me to the hole under the tree stump and started digging. I began to be showered with soil and had to move as the excavation works got more and more frantic.

Later that day, both terriers began to trail behind Sitka. They were both tired and wanted a lift so I picked both up and put them in their saddlebags. We were ambling along at Sitka's slow pace, when out of the corner of my eye I saw a brown terrier walking along beside me. At first, I just assumed it was Russet, but no, it couldn't be; he was in the saddlebag. It had a collar but there wasn't a name tag on it. "Go home. Go home!" I shouted at it, but it had no intention of going home and still followed us. Russet and Pippin kept stretching their necks out of their saddlebags to see it. We were coming to a busy road. There was no way I could have three terriers on Sitka. What should I do?

There was a cottage on the roadside just where we needed to turn onto the busier road, so I knocked on the door. A lady answered the door, "Oh, you've got Benjie following you. He comes from the farm way down the road." I explained I wasn't sure what to do but fortunately she said she would keep him and take him home later.

It was 11th November by the time we got to my sister's house in Buxton and we still had a lot of miles to cover before getting home.

After a couple of days rest, we continued on our way. The weather was awful; so wet and miserable. We plodded on – all four of us not feeling at all enthusiastic. By late evening even the daylight seemed to have lost enthusiasm to continue on. It began to get dark as the black clouds rolled in. The rain did eventually stop, but we had all had enough. I could see a farm ahead of us right on the roadside. It would be handy if we could stay there. We turned into the yard and went up to the farmhouse door and knocked. A cat shot past us and a collie barked frantically at us. Ducks and bantams were in the yard, but no sign of a person. I looked around the buildings, and called out, but no one answered. If we waited it would get darker and darker and there was no guarantee anyone would turn up so we plodded on wearily looking for the next farm. It seemed a long way on but at least I knew we could stay there because I had camped there before and had always been told I was welcome any time. It was getting darker and darker and it was raining again.

We only just made it. "It's too dark and wet to pitch a tent tonight. Go into the barn for the night. There is plenty of grass in the paddock behind the barn for your pony." I had been in the barn before. It had a row of cow stalls on one side, a channel down the centre for all the muck and pee to collect from the beasts tied by old cow chains into each stall but the other side was a plain concrete area wide enough for me to lay my sleeping bag out and have my saddlebags alongside.

If the cattle were still outside, camping in there was fine, but having camped in there before with cattle backsides facing towards me all pooing and peeing throughout the night, there was no avoiding being splattered up from the poo and pee landing on past poo and pee already in that channel between the beasts and me. Yes, unfortunately the cattle were inside. The dogs were alright as they were down at the bottom of the sleeping bag all night. Even with the saddlebags as a barrier, I could feel the damp splashes hitting my face every so often and a strong smell of poo. Fortunately there was plenty of rain to wash off the cow splatters from my face next morning. I could hear the rain on the barn roof as I woke up. I led Sitka into the barn to saddle up and put all the packs on him. Neither Pippin or Russet wanted to face the day. They could hear the rain even down my sleeping bag. I had to tip the sleeping bag up and tip them out!

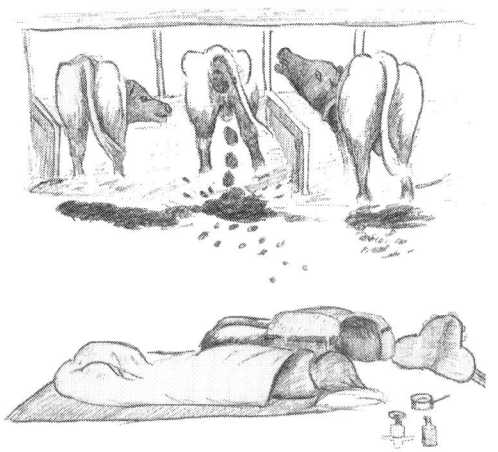

We were into the Yorkshire Dales when at last we got a fine day as we made our way to Gargrave to call on a lovely lady I first met in 1973 when Sitka and I made our very first trip south. She had seen us passing on a cold wet day and invited me in for a bowl of soup and gave Sitka a bucket of oats in a stable next to her house. We always got a lovely welcome whenever we called to see her.

By the time we got to Gargrave it was late afternoon. "Why don't you put Sitka in the paddock and come and stay in the house?" There was a pony in the paddock lying flat out. I could see from the shape of its feet it had laminitis so was lying down because its feet were sore. Pippin couldn't make out why it wouldn't get up and bounced around it yapping until I dragged her away. Once it saw Sitka it did get up and hobble towards him. It was so excited to see another horse. Sitka was too hungry to bother about greeting it. When I went to check if they were alright later that evening, it was following Sitka around on its overgrown feet.

Sitka seemed to be feeling the urgency to get home before the weather got worse and the days got even shorter. He began to really step out at a faster pace, so we managed to get to another farm where we had camped in previous years. The grass was poor and there was so much sheep poo about I couldn't avoid putting my tent on some. Sitka looked at me after sniffing at the sheepy grass as if to tell me it wasn't good enough for him to eat - so with Russet and Pippin I walked back to the farm and was given a sack of hay.

Next morning the tent was covered in ice and it was bitterly cold. As the dogs and I snuggled down in the sleeping bag we hoped the sun might eventually come up. Sitka was calling for more hay. There was no sign of any sunshine; even if there had been it was really too late in the year for it to have much heat; we had to move on. The tent wouldn't fit in the bag with all the ice on it. I shook it and shook it. Slithers of ice like thin glass kept falling off it. Even then, I struggled with frozen hands to wrap it tight enough to get into its bag so it would fit in the back of Sitka's saddle.

It was a cold miserable day but not cold enough to stop the ice still on the tent from thawing with the heat from Sitka's back. The wet from melted ice oozed through the tent bag and down onto the saddle blanket under the saddle. The dogs and I had a wet saddle blanket to sit on in the tent that night.

We had camped near Langthwaite. The rain got heavier and heavier through the night. Next morning all was quiet, no sound of rain, no wind howling and no ice on the tent. Even the sun was peering over the hills as we set off. We had a ford to cross ahead of us, so I got on Sitka to let him carry me over it, leaving both terriers to find their own way across.

As Sitka stepped into the water, I suddenly realised it was a bit deeper than I expected. I saw Russet walk into the water then start swimming. There was a yelp from Pippin, then a splash as she leapt into the water, then with those little legs working as fast as they could, she followed

Russet across the river. Later that day we had another ford to cross; I could see it wasn't that deep. The terriers could both manage to walk across – but no – Pippin wasn't going to chance it this time so I turned Sitka back towards the bank where she was sitting crying to see if I could stretch over and pick her up without getting off. As Sitka stopped ready for me to reach down and grab her, she jumped up onto his backside and stood there as we crossed back over again. This became a regular habit whenever we crossed a ford; as long as there was a reasonably high bank for her to take off from and I got Sitka close enough to it, up she jumped.

It was a bit of a wet weary trudge the rest of the way home. The grass was very poor and Sitka had been constantly telling me over those last few days that he needed more good grass. Whenever he saw a patch of better grass, he kept pulling me towards it and I would have to drag him on and away from it. Then on that last day, November 24th, he suddenly realised we were nearly home and he forgot about pulling me towards areas of good grass. His walking pace increased and he was pulling me towards home.

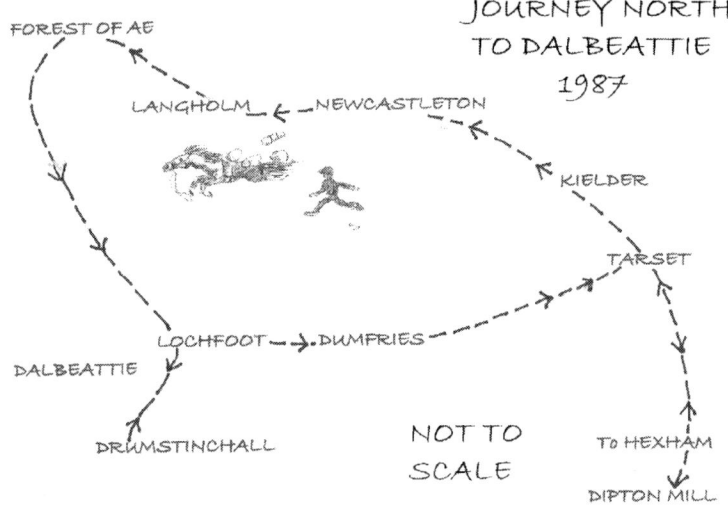

3

JOURNEY NORTH TO DALBEATTIE WITH ORIEL, RUSSET & TINKER

Summer 1987

We were now in 1987. Sitka would be 21 years old on April 9th. The sarcoid that was causing him trouble with his waterworks had got worse. Jester was a strong three-year-old; when he and Sitka were playing together in the field it was hard to tell the difference between them but I knew Jester was still too young and inexperienced to take over Sitka's role as pack pony for another year at least. Would Sitka be able to do another journey south? I was mulling over thoughts of venturing into Devon in the autumn. What about Sitka's daughter Oriel? She was a beautiful mare I had bred from one of the riding school fell ponies back in Sitka's days as a stallion. Her only problem was her terrible fear of speeding traffic. I would ride her down into Hexham and take her through the main street a few times and see how she behaved.

There is no doubt animals can sense how you feel and respond accordingly. I was determined she would face that traffic, and she did. We repeated those trips through the town, so the next challenge was getting her to accept saddlebags on her back. I filled two sacks of hay and slung them over the saddle, then led her up the field. All went well at first, then something startled her and the sacks thumped her side. She was off full belt across the field and over the next fence and into the woods still with the sacks thumping her sides. The more those sacks bumped her sides, the faster and further she went until soon she was out of sight.

It was pointless running after her, so I went back to the house and collected a bucket with some feed in it and a halter in case she had snapped the bridle when getting the reins caught on something, when I heard the phone ring. "It's Jack Dinning speaking. There is a loose pony in my field next to the woods with a saddle on it. Could it be one of yours?"

"Yes, it will be," and I told him what had happened so he was reassured that no one had fallen off and was lying injured somewhere. It was a half hour walk to get to where she was and she must have jumped over another fence to get there, then the sacks must have fallen off, and she was grazing peacefully in Jack's field.

I led her home, tied her in the stable and got two more sacks stuffed with hay and put them over her back and left her tied up with them on her. Eventually, we progressed with having real saddlebags on her with me on her as well. Then I started taking her on a day's journey to see some friends near Brampton in Cumbria, stayed there overnight and riding her back next day.

***

The next plan was to ride her over to see Catherine in Dumfriesshire, stay there a few days then ride her home again. That meant a three or four day trip with all the camping gear and two terriers. In the meantime Sitka was running out with Jester between his duties as a riding school pony. He looked really well apart from the wretched growth into his 'water works' which the vet warned me would eventually cause a blockage so that he couldn't pee.

The two of them would race around the field and every so often Pippin would join in the fun; it was a dangerous game she was really forbidden to play. One of those hooves catching her could kill her but being a Jack Russell terrier, the temptation was too great; fear never entered her little head. Then one day as I was stopping her trying to play the dangerous game, a rabbit ran across the field. Russet saw it and he was off after it in full cry. Pippin heard him and decided that sounded exciting and was off after him and they both disappeared down the bank into the woods. I left them to it. "They'll be back soon," I thought.

After about twenty minutes Russet appeared but no Pippin. With Russet following we set out to the woods to look for her. I called and called and tried to get Russet to show me where she was. I trudged up and down the bank calling her name down the rabbit holes, remembering well that this was where Russet had disappeared three years ago.

Later that evening, there was still no Pippin. I feared the worst. Next day a variety of friends arrived with spades and we all attacked as many rabbit holes as we could find but it was hopeless. Tree roots and stones prevented us from digging far. All we could do was yell "Pippin!" down each hole after digging as far as we could.

Weeks passed and all hope faded. After a month all hope was completely lost. What a tragic end to such a young life. She was only two years old and such a lovely little character ….. but terriers will be terriers. Keeping them on leads or restricted completely from any freedom would be cruel.

Oriel was still doing well with her training as a pack pony. I had Russet in his saddlebag when we were on the roads and made two more two-day trips to Brampton. We were now ready to make our two week journey to Dalbeattie in Dumfriesshire. I wasn't going to risk going through Dumfries with its very busy roads so we would go by the Ae Forest then down to Lochfoot, just west of Dumfries. From there to Drumstinchal where we could be on quiet roads. I had trained Oriel to tether; she quickly got used to the rope so as not to get it twisted round her legs. That meant I didn't have to worry while I was in the tent at night, always listening in case she got tangled and panicked.

Our first day went well. We camped at Tarset, then the next day went through Kielder Forest and avoided meeting any Forestry wagons leading timber. Wherever one goes, there is no avoiding some roads. Unfortunately, we came to a road that had just been redone with tarmac then stone chippings on top. A notice said "Slow loose chippings," but drivers seemed to be taking no heed of the notice. One car flew past us at speed sending loose chipping from its wheels. Oriel was flinching from the speed it went but when loose chippings went from the wheels and hit her, that was too much for her. If I hadn't been leading her at the time, I might have managed to control her but I had got off to put Russet in his saddlebag as we came to the road, and had decided to walk a short distance to stretch my legs before getting on again.

The reins were wrenched out of my hands and with Russet in his saddlebag, my pack pony was gone at a flat-out gallop. Another car raced by and I thought "Sod it, why couldn't the driver have stopped?" I ran down the road and saw a grass track leading off to the road. From the hoof prints it looked like she had turned off the road down the track.

It didn't take me long to see she had gone down the track. I hadn't gone far when I discovered bits of my camping gear, the saddlebags, then the saddle and saddle blanket and poor old Russet lying on the ground but no sign of Oriel. Russet looked a bit dazed but was alright so we walked on together when suddenly, there was a man leading Oriel towards us.

"I was in the car behind you when I saw your horse bolt and turn down the track. I knew the track led back onto the road so drove quickly on to the other end of the track to stop it from bolting back onto the road," he told me, as I was realising that must have been the car that shot past me just after she bolted. How grateful was I for his quick reactions? He handed me Oriel and off he went back to his car.

I led her back to where all my things were strewn out along the track and tied her to a gate then gathered everything into a pile. Fortunately, the sun was shining so Russet and I sat down and he watched me trying to sort everything out and try to decide what to do next. The situation looked hopeless but I had to do something. So, I sorted out everything into two piles – one pile of things that although damaged, were still workable, then another pile of things that would have to have an emergency repair somehow. Nothing seemed to be missing and the emergency sewing kit with extra straps and lots of boot laces was still in one of the saddle bags so out it came and I set to work.

It was the afternoon and the sun continued to shine. The grass track was wide so I reasoned that if I didn't get all the packs repaired enough to get back onto Oriel in time to move on that day, we could camp on a wide space at the side of the track for the night.

It took several hours of sewing, tying things together with boot laces and fastening together with extra straps by the time I got all useable items onto Oriel's back. We still had a few hours of daylight left and I did want to get Oriel back into her pack pony duties as soon as possible.

With Russet in his saddlebag and me mounted on her back, we set off onto the road ahead and continued on. We managed to get to Drumstinchall some days later without mishaps. Poor Oriel, with the nervous tension of it all on top of all those miles of carrying Russet, me and all the packs she had lost so much weight she looked like a big greyhound rather than a chunky cob.

After a few days rest at Catherine's, she looked more relaxed and had put on a bit of weight. Our journey home was less traumatic. I made sure I was mounted on her whenever we were on roads. A group of motorcyclists roaring past us had us charging down the road one day. It took me a while to get Oriel to slow down because I was frightened Russet was going to be chucked out of his saddlebag, so was trying to hold on to him with one hand as well as one rein which means not being able to use both reins together properly.

We got safely back home, but I decided Oriel was not going to be a suitable pack pony to go all the way to Devon that autumn.

We hadn't been home long when a friend arrived at the yard and said "Jane, there's an advert in the local paper for a ten week old Jack Russell bitch puppy," and gave me the telephone number from the advert! Two days later a farmer from Haltwhistle arrived with a lovely black and white puppy he called Tinker.

Jester was now three years old. I had started lunging him and had even had a saddle on him and been on his back myself. He was also learning well to be tethered on a long rope which I had tied on an old railway sleeper so that if he did get the rope caught round a leg and began to pull to get free the sleeper would move so he didn't get a rope burn. Gradually he was learning how to avoid getting the rope tangled round his legs. He looked strong and well grown enough to take on the role of pack pony but I knew he had to be at least four years old and developed enough to take on the task.

4

JOURNEY SOUTH TO DEVON WITH SITKA, RUSSET & TINKER

Autumn 1987

Could Sitka do another journey? He looked fit enough but what about that wretched sarcoid which was gradually getting bigger? I decided to get the vet to give him a thorough check out and see what he advised. "His heart and lungs are in good order for a horse of his age. The sarcoid doesn't seem to be causing him any pain or distress yet. If you are only walking and leading him I don't see any problem in you going all the way to Devon and back again," which I was very pleased to hear.

It was the end of the school summer holidays; a very busy time for the riding school. It was difficult to find time to get the camping gear ready and pack the saddlebags. Then there were Sitka's shoes to put on, with extra welding on the toes and heels so they would last longer. Somehow Tinker's training to sit in the saddlebag never got started. She was an energetic puppy but learned very quickly. She didn't have the usual Jack Russell attitude of "I'll do it my way!" I felt sure she would be no trouble if I just picked her up and put her in the saddlebag when she needed to be in it.

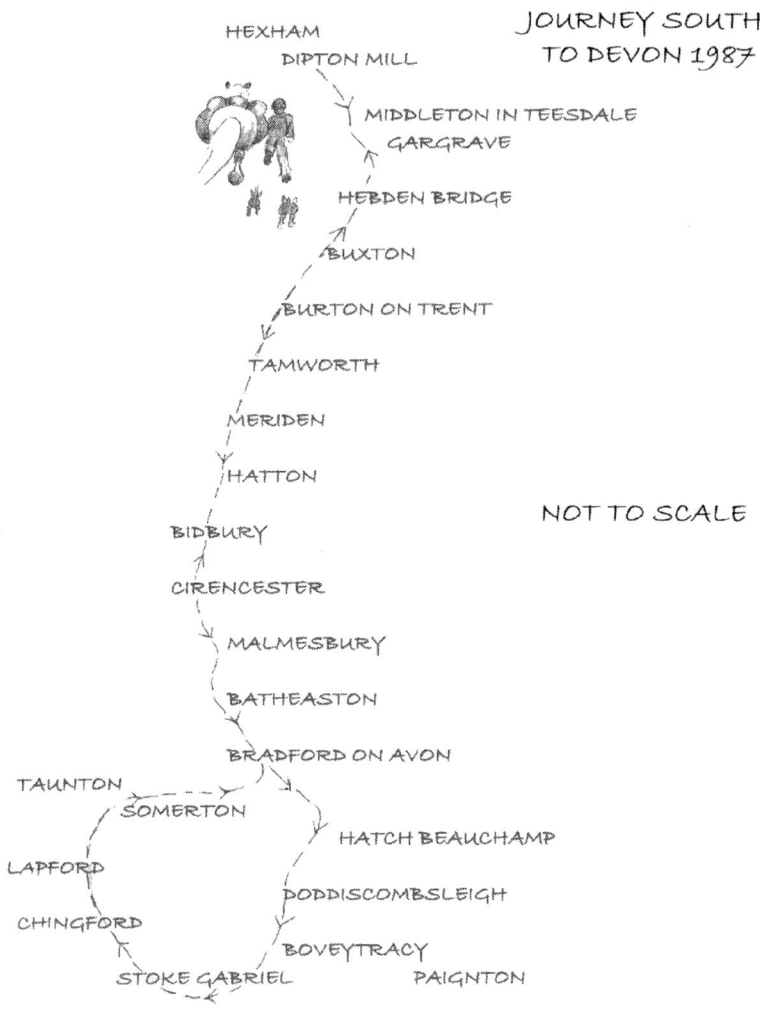

As soon as Russet saw the saddlebags, he knew what was about to happen. Then once he saw Sitka being tacked up and the saddlebags being put on him, he started to yap with excitement. Tinker sat watching not at all sure what all the fuss was about.

It had been a very wet summer. I was hoping that we may have got a dry autumn. Our first two days were good; we even had some sun on the second day as we got into the Yorkshire Dales. Tinker soon got used to being in the saddlebag although she did look awkward the first time I put her into it. She couldn't get comfortable and wriggled about pushing herself up with her back legs then trying to lie on Sitka's neck. I kept pushing her back into the saddlebag but each time she would try to lie with her front paws over Sitka's neck.

Eventually, I realised she was standing on her back legs rather than sitting in it. Her back legs were getting tired so she pushed herself up on Sitka's neck to lie on it. That was fine until I got to a gate all tied up with baler twine so I let go of Sitka's reins to untie it. Sitka immediately put his head down to graze and Tinker slipped down his neck.

It took some time for her to learn to relax and sit in the saddlebag. I had to keep pushing her down into it then after several attempts of trying to get her to sit she finally got the message and the back legs folded up and she sat inside her saddlebag and realised she could go to sleep in it.

There are an awful lot of cattle grids in the North Yorkshire Dales. That meant taking Sitka through the side gate alongside. Many of them are not used much and are tied up with string or dropping to pieces. On one the local farmer had tied old tyres onto an old gate to stop his sheep from escaping. I couldn't get the gate to open with all those tyres hanging on it, so was struggling to get some of the tyres off it when I heard a yelp behind me and turned round. There was Tinker in the cattle grid; she had dropped through between the bars and couldn't get back through them. I could just get my hands between the bars of the grid and get hold of her, but it seemed impossible to get her back through. Next, I tried pulling her through by her front legs, but her head got stuck. So, I had to let her go and she dropped back in the grid. Then kneeling on the bars, I grabbed her front legs with one hand then with the other hand guided her head in the right direction. Hurray, she came out!!! "Don't you dare drop back into it, Tinker!" I told her as I put her down well away from the grid and continued to struggle with the gate.

The ground was still very wet after such a wet summer even though we had had such fine days since we set off; and that night it rained heavily. Unfortunately some of the tracks already had standing water on them. Next morning when we set off, the rain had stopped but the ground was very wet and there was a lot more standing water to paddle through along the tracks.

Russet had mastered the art of jumping up onto a wall alongside the flooded track and walking along the top of the wall to avoid the deep water. Both Russet and Tinker were out of their saddlebags as we walked along a grass track when we came to a flooded area. Sitka and I were splashing through the water then I noticed Russet on the wall alongside us, but where was Tinker? I looked back and there she was on the wall looking very unsafe but slowly following him, walking along on the top stones of the wall. How she had managed to get up onto the wall I wasn't sure. I doubted she could have jumped up but she had got up there somehow and managed to keep up with Russet until we got past the flooded area. Then Russet jumped down again, so I lifted Tinker down rather than let her jump landing on such young legs from such a height.

Our progress was awfully slow. Sitka's walking pace seemed to be that of a very weary horse. Was it all too much for him, despite what the vet had said? He had had a busy summer doing riding school work.

We continued on into Derbyshire and down through old Buxton to the Ashbourne railway line, the Tissington Trail, where both dogs could be out of their saddlebags. All Tinker wanted to do was play with Russet, but he objected and got cross with her. There were no rabbits about; Russet had tried his best to find one and had had his nose down, but not found even the scent of one.

Tinker was walking beside me as I tried to urge Sitka to walk a bit faster. Russet was ahead of us but we were going so slowly, he stopped and turned round to see if we were still moving, then he came bouncing up to Sitka and grabbed the end of the reins I was holding. It was a game he used to play as a puppy and continued when he got older. When I led the ponies from their fields at home with a rope halter, he loved to grab the end of the rope and pull the ponies along himself. He hadn't played the game for several years but we were going so slowly he must have got bored – no rabbits to hunt so he grabbed Sitka's reins and decided to pull him along; however it didn't increase Sitka's pace. I felt as if Tinker and I should be behind and pushing him along while Russet pulled him.

No. I decided that really there was nothing wrong with Sitka, he was just an old man who had done these journeys over so many years and now found it all a bit boring, and like us all as we get a lot older, we tire far more easily. He remembered all the places where we had stopped either to camp or to have a picnic and where he could graze. As soon as he recognised we were near one of these places, his pace increased rapidly until we were at the actual spot he knew he had stopped in past years and was able to graze. I had used the same route down into Warwickshire regularly from the very first trip south with Sitka in 1973, so he knew it well, but from Warwickshire we had always gone into Oxfordshire then headed for the Sussex Downs. This time we were going towards Bath to visit Ainslie at Batheaston then on to Devon.

It was Ainslie who inspired me to do that very first journey south with Sitka to visit her when she moved from Hexham to live near Batheaston. The bridleways marked on my maps had improved a lot since that first journey south in 1973. Many were fenced off or had padlocked gates across them back then but had now been made more accessible for horses thanks to the British Horse Society and local councils.

We got down to the Cotswolds, and a lady assured me I could get along the Cotswold Way with a horse. She had done it herself. I soon found that it really should have been with a horse that could jump stiles but somehow we managed to find a way around by finding gates into nearby fields then more gates to get us back onto the tracks. It got very frustrating but at last we got through and didn't have to turn back which would have been even more frustrating. Also, Russet and Tinker enjoyed the freedom out of their saddlebags where they had been confined a lot of the way in Warwickshire where we couldn't avoid being on busy roads.

Our provisions were getting low. We had passed through many villages. Most of them had a house called 'The Old Post Office', but none had a Post Office selling groceries any more. We ended up going into Cirencester as I had no dog food left at all, which was serious! Sitka had to share my porridge oats; they were the only oats I had left. He found that the porridge oats on their own got stuck in his teeth; if I put chopped carrots into the nose bag with his porridge oats, they prevented that from happening which was disappointing for Tinker. She had decided bits of chewed porridge oats falling from Sitka's mouth onto the ground were good to lick up and eat. After I took the nosebag off Sitka's head, he would flick his tongue out of his mouth, and try and get of all the oats that were stuck on his teeth. A lot ended up on Tinker as she stood underneath his head searching for bits that had fallen onto the grass.

We were picnicking one day on the old Roman Road north of Bath – the Fosseway. A lot of it has been converted into a horrid busy main road, but there are still bits of it left as grass tracks. I remembered it back in 1973, but what a mess people had made of it since then. There was fly-tipped rubbish in the ditch at the sides. We met a council worker collecting various items along the track; I stopped to chat to him as he was struggling to get what looked like a freezer out of the ditch. He complained, "I cannot understand why folk have to dump this rubbish here. All they have to do is ring the Council and have it collected!"

It took me a while to find a good grass area for Sitka to graze where there was no dumped rubbish so we could stop for lunch. Russet and Tinker shared my bread and cheese then Russet suddenly rushed to a nearby mole hill. The earth was moving, so the mole must have been digging underneath. Tinker sat watching Russet who made a quick dive at the moving molehill then dug frantically into it but it was too late. The mole must have gone and Russet, soil all over his face, gave up then looked at me. I could see he was ready to get going again, so we continued on and got to Batheaston that night.

***

Sitka had a well-deserved rest for a few days while we stayed with Ainslie at her farm near Batheaston.

Tinker had a great time playing with Ainslie's Labrador puppy. Russet kept right out of the way of the energetic young things and found the best chair in the large kitchen to jump up on and make himself comfortable.

I had my maps on the kitchen table to try and find a route south into Devon avoiding main roads. There were very few bridleways marked on the maps and any that were marked seemed to only get us back onto main roads again. In the end I decided to stick to the yellow unclassified roads by Ashley and Bradford-on-Avon, then by Great Elm.

Tinker had been doing a lot of scratching. Did she have fleas? I wasn't sure but I decided to give her an anti-flea wash before we left. As it was a sunny morning I could wash her outside and she would soon dry out in the sun. Poor Tinker; she was horrified at being put in a bowl of water then anti-flea shampoo rubbed into her coat followed by several rinses. She tried hard to escape whenever she thought she had a chance. When well rinsed I let her go; she shot off and ran madly round and round shaking herself before setting off again running round in circles until she felt she had got rid of most of the wet.

After the ordeal she decided she wasn't going to come near me; even when coaxed with titbits she decided it was too risky. She wasn't going to be washed again.

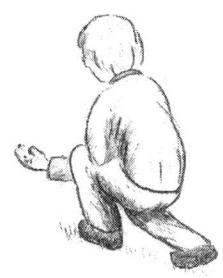

Next day I was planning to set off again. Sitka had had a good rest; the weather forecast was good and I had my route marked on the maps. We were heading into new territory. I needed to be able to rely on following the route marked on my map, which could be so difficult if it was raining. The map cover would get wet and my glasses would be covered in raindrops making it nearly impossible to read the map.

I got Sitka all packed up and Russet was barking with excitement as he knew well we were about to be off on our travels again but Tinker was still keeping her distance from me and sat watching Russet yapping, not sure whether she wanted to join us or not.

Those yellow unclassified roads marked on my map, which I thought would be quiet country roads, were very narrow and far from quiet. It wasn't until a car driver opened his window and shouted at me as he nearly hit us, "I didn't expect to meet you round the corner. You shouldn't be on the road, it's too dangerous!" Of course, it was commuter time, people dashing to work and he was telling me I was a danger for him, not he was a danger for me!

We camped that night on a farm belonging to a lady farmer who had a herd of Guernsey cattle. It was a relief to get in a field away from the traffic. The roads had got quieter after the commuter rush but then we had to dodge out of the way of farmers' tractors and machinery, which took up the whole width of the narrow roads.

Next day it was back to more vehicles speeding along the roads. The banks on each side of the road were high and impossible to walk on, to get out of the way of any vehicles, which meant we had to find a gateway. Impatient drivers hooted their horns at us. I was beginning to feel fed up when there ahead of us was a grass track. Yes, I could go along and join the road again later, a local farmer told me. Parked at the side further down the track was a double decker bus converted into a 'house' with someone living in it! I had to persuade Sitka it wasn't moving, or about to move, to get him past it.

Later that day I planned to try a bridleway marked on the map. There was a field full of horses right by the spot where the bridleway started. Surely if there are horses about, riders will ride down local bridleways, but no. We got several yards down the track to find it blocked by overgrown bushes. I led Sitka back and called at the house near the field full of horses. "No, the bridleway is blocked; we don't clear it as the bushes provide shelter for the field," she told me.

Back to roads again until we got to a place called Birchwood where another short bridleway was marked on my map but it was all blocked with overgrown brambles and gorse bushes. So once again it was back to the roads.

Not far away was another place with horses grazing and I saw a lady in the yard. She blamed the local authorities at Taunton and Yeovil for neglecting the bridleways; I wondered where these horsey people ride their horses. The roads were awful with so much traffic on them and huge banks on each side, which were impossible to get onto to get out of the driver's way.

We had got to the very attractive village of Bickleigh and then onto a back road towards Tiverton. It was getting late, just as I was wondering where I was going to camp, a van came up alongside and a young man called out "Would you like a place to camp for the night?" He explained that he had a paddock behind the house with nothing in it and I was welcome to stop there. It was only another mile or so along the road, he told me.

Sitka was tired, both dogs were fed up of being in their saddlebags and unable to get out for a run, and I was becoming more and more annoyed with continually having to find a gateway to get out of the way of impatient drivers. None were prepared to reverse into a space they had just passed. They would stop then expect me to lead Sitka back to a gateway we had just passed so progress was very slow. The young fellow's directions led us to a house surrounded by junk. He came out to meet us and pointed to his paddock, which was really a steep sloping bank behind the house. "We'll have to go through the neighbour's field," he said and led the way. I couldn't help wondering what the neighbours

thought about all the rubbish next to them. "There is a level bit up at the top of the bank which should be suitable for you to pitch your tent," he said, pointing up a very steep slope.

Sitka put his brakes on and refused to be led up so I took off his bridle and walked up to the top with Russet and Tinker who thought 'this is great – there are loads of rabbit burrows!' They were at the top long before I was, inspecting each burrow as they went. Once Sitka realised we were going to leave him, I knew he would follow us. He stood and watched us for a while then gave a loud neigh, forgot all about being tired, then charged up the bank to join us.

"Will that do?" I heard a voice call out from away below.

"Yes thanks, it will do fine!" I called back, but thinking it was only just wide enough to pitch a tent.

Next day we reached a village called Drewsteignton. Ahead of me was a group of horses with riders on them looking very well dressed. It must be a hunt meet, I thought, so decided to stop and watch for a while. More horses arrived all beautifully turned out. Yes, it had to be a hunt meet. A small crowd of people arrived, then a police car. I saw the policeman go up to the group of people and usher them away.

Sitka was watching the horses; he knew about hunting, as I had ridden him with the local farmers' hunt back at home a few times. I didn't want him to think I was going to join in the hunt, so I kept hold of him at a distance from them. We couldn't go on because they were blocking the way we wanted to go. Suddenly I realised two policemen were behind us. "You'll have to move on, you cannot stay here." They sounded quite aggressive and wouldn't accept my reason for waiting for a while until the horses moved away. Eventually they believed me when I told them what I was doing travelling with a pack pony. Then they explained there had been a lot of trouble with anti-bloodsport people attacking riders at local meets.

I led Sitka forward to continue on but by the terrible looks I got from the riders on their horses they didn't believe I was not a protestor.

Later that day we were near Chagford when a lady came running up to me with her camera. "Would you let me take a photograph of your pony with the two dogs on it?"

I stopped Sitka then stood back so both dogs could be seen but no, that wouldn't do, she wanted the photograph with her cottage in the background. She pointed to the small cottage on the roadside so I led Sitka back towards it and turned him around again trying to make sure both dogs could be seen in their saddlebags.

Eventually she got her photograph and we continued on towards Widecombe, expecting to have to continue on the road, then I saw a track ahead. I looked at the map. It did mark a bridleway heading right into Widecombe. It looked a well trodden track – Russet and Tinker could get out of their saddlebags at last and we could stop and picnic away from the road.

I had a tin of dog meat for Russet and Tinker to share so emptied it giving half to Russet and the rest to Tinker, then put the tin on the ground intending to squash the sides in before we went on so it would fit in my small rubbish bag to put in the next village litter bin.

Tinker saw the empty tin and decided she needed to lick out the meat at the bottom of it, but couldn't get it back off her head. I watched her; she looked so ridiculous, then I got up and held onto the tin to try and pull it off her head but it was so firmly stuck it wouldn't move. The more I pulled the more I pulled Tinker along with the tin.

In the end, I had to hold Tinker between my legs then pull the tin until it eventually came off her head.

**

We arrived at Widecombe just as a thunderstorm started. The rain sloshed down but we managed to get a bit of shelter by the church until the heaviest rain eased. We carried on to Cockingford where the owner of a campsite let us into a field he was no longer using, as it was the end of the caravan and camping season. It was a lovely peaceful spot in a beautiful area. We had got as far as I had marked out on my map. I had planned that if I got to Devon in time, I would go to an International Bible Study Assembly in Paignton but now the thought of having to adapt to coping with a few days in a town was worrying me. I knew I would regret it if I didn't make the effort to go as planned because it was the countryside and its wildlife that I loved to be in, and that led me to query what the Bible revealed.

As a child, going to church was a boring ordeal my sister and I had to put up with each Sunday because it was considered by my parents as the right thing to do. It was in later years when I rode my fell pony into the woods or onto the fells and see the wildlife, that convinced me there was a designer behind it all. Then watching the swallows nesting in the rafters of the old stone barn, the roe deer in the woods, the curlews, the plovers, the grouse up on the fells all had their basic pattern of living.

The swallows all made sounds like swallows, they all flew like swallows, made nests like swallows make, and all ate what swallows eat. The roe deer in the woods, the curlews, the plovers and the grouse on the fells all had their set basic patterns of living. Curlews all sounded and behaved like curlews, plovers' basic actions and reactions were those of plovers, and so it was with the grouse and also with all the other living things I heard and saw. Each individual species had its basic pattern of living instilled into it, unlike like the human species.

Those people I knew who were coming from the north to attend the Bible Study Assembly had chosen to come to Devon, some by car, some by bus, others by train and were to stay in hotels and guest houses. I had chosen to walk with a pack pony carrying my accommodation and relying on maps to guide me the right way.

The swallows I saw gathering on the telephone lines before I left home would be well on their way to Africa. Even the youngest ones who had never left home would be on their way and often left after the parent birds. No maps to guide them. They went the way that swallows are programmed to go with the ability to get there already in them.

It all fascinated me and I was convinced that all life was designed and created by a super-being for a purpose. As far as I could work out in my simple mind, if a being had designed and created all, then it is vastly greater than us; an argument I am sure many, if not most, would soon trample on with more intellectual reasoning than mine.

Yes, I would go on towards Paignton and see if I could find a place to camp for a few days and on a bus route into the town so I can go there and back and not be away from Sitka and the dogs for too long.

I got the map of the area and spread it out on the ground when we picnicked near Stoke Gabriel. We had passed lots of Caravan Club sites on farms, but none wanted a pony and a tent on them. All other camp sites seemed to be closed as it was the end of the season. I marked my map with a route around the area off main roads and we set off again.

Not far from Stoke Gabriel, I saw a farm with lots of caravans in a large field with a notice pointing to a paddock 'Tents Only,' but no tents pitched on it. We went into the farmyard and met a man coming out of the farmhouse. He laughed at the sight of the two terriers sitting in their saddlebags on Sitka. I explained to him what I wanted and he stood saying nothing for a moment, then said "I can see no reason why you can't go into the tent area. The season is over and there is plenty grass for your pony for a few days. The washroom by the caravan site is open as there are still a few caravanners. You can use it, will that do?"

I was very grateful and just got the tent up when down came the rain. The dogs needed a walk before we settled in the tent. Tinker was full of energy as the 'quiet' side roads we had been on were far from quiet. There was that rush of traffic as commuters dashed home to their country dwellings. A notice saying 'Public footpath to Stoke Gabriel' was by the caravan field. We could walk there and get provisions but Russet refused to leave the tent, so Tinker and I left him asleep on the saddle blanket and walked down the footpath, got provisions, then walked back and joined Russet in the tent. I had managed to gather lots of mushrooms on the way and again on the way back so supper was a pan full of mushrooms fried in butter with chunks of cheese mixed in with them.

I got a bus timetable while in Stoke Gabriel so the next morning I tried to look less like someone who had been camping for several weeks and left both dogs behind and caught a bus into Paignton. I found the hall where the Assembly was, then struggled to cope with the hot, stuffy atmosphere and keep alert and listening, but it was difficult. I kept nodding off to sleep.

It was Thursday 15th October, a terrible wet day. This was my last day in Paignton so I got provisions ready for setting off the next morning on our trip homeward, before catching the bus back to the camp site.

Russet and Tinker were pleased to see me but neither of them wanted to come out of the tent into the wet as the rain poured down. Sitka greeted me with his usual whinnying but seemed very restless. I went over to give him some of the carrots I had bought in Paignton then dragged Russet and Tinker out of the tent and walked down the public footpath where I gathered lots more mushrooms to cook for my supper. The rain had no intention of stopping. The three of us were glad to get back in the tent, but why was Sitka so restless and kept calling to me?

It got dark early so after going out to check if Sitka's waterproof sheet was still firmly in place and making the dogs come out for a final pee, we settled down for the night. I had noticed how windy it was when taking the dogs for their walk down the public footpath but back at our camp spot all seemed calm. It wasn't until later in the night that I woke up hearing a roar like an express train speeding past us then another and another. The tent shuddered violently with each roar as the wind hit it with sudden blasts.

After a while I decided I had better check that the tent pegs hadn't come loose or we would end up with the tent blown down and all that wet soaking in. Eventually I had to brave it and go out to push the tent pegs firmly back into the ground. Sitka was standing with his back to the rain and gale. I was thankful he still had his waterproof sheet firmly on. The wind appeared to get even stronger. I had to brave it and go out a second time to push the tent pegs back firmly into the ground.

By morning all had become quiet. I peered out of the tent to check Sitka was still there; he was grazing peacefully. I put on my pocket radio for the weather forecast and the news. There was a shocking report of the havoc caused by last night's violent gale; roads blocked by fallen trees and floods and police warning not to take a vehicle out onto the roads unless absolutely necessary.

When I got out of the tent and looked across to where the caravans were, what a shock I got. There were caravans on their sides and some completely smashed up. I had noticed last night no one seemed to be on the site as there were no cars there. We had been fortunate; the high hedge and trees round the paddock we were camping in had given us some shelter.

Once we set off again, I realised why there had been the police warning on the radio. Trees and huge branches were everywhere; at least we could manage to get round or over all of them but it would have been hopeless in a vehicle. It did have an advantage for me for most of the day – the roads were so quiet; no vehicles at all until later in the afternoon. Even then they were going slowly as drivers were so cautious with all the branches still lying on the roads.

Progress was slow as we had to keep stopping to move branches off the road. My plan was to go and visit old family friends in Tiverton but we were not going to get there that night. I rang them up from a telephone box. They would meet me next day at Doddiscombsleigh at Nobody's Inn and we could have lunch there together. I was glad to see when I got there that there was a good grass area where I could tether Sitka to graze. After lunch they wanted me to go back with them to see their house in Tiverton. The owner of the pub said I could pitch my tent on the grass area where Sitka was tethered and he would keep an eye on it and Sitka while I was away.

Russet jumped into the car, but Tinker had never been in a car since she came to me. She was terrified as the engine started and the car moved. Russet was happily sitting on my knee looking out of the car window but Tinker crept between my legs on the floor then was sick over my feet - we had to stop and with a handful of grass I tried to clean my boots. Poor Tinker, she was very unhappy even when we arrived and went into the house. They tried to persuade me to stay the night but I managed to persuade them I needed to get back to see that Sitka was safe and to get Tinker back while she was empty so hopefully not sick in the car again.

It was a much happier Tinker that got out of the car and saw Sitka and the tent.

I wanted to see some of Dartmoor while we were in Devon so went by Hatch Beauchamp, passing a large house called Hatch Court where a huge deer stood and watched us. It stared at Sitka with the packs on him, or maybe it was the dogs in the saddlebags that had it standing watching us for so long. We stood and watched it for a while until it decided that was enough, turned and walked steadily away from us.

Sitka had now had so many years of journeys as a pack pony, he had got used to most sights and sounds and put up with most vehicles on the roads, but as we were on our way to Somerton and going over a railway bridge, one of the Intercity 125 express trains appeared from nowhere and shot under the bridge just as we were on it. It was a long time since I had seen the old fellow move so quickly!

It was a few days later when Sitka had another frightening experience. A huge high wagon passed us on a narrow road; we had only just managed to get out of the way when there was a loud bang. The top of the vehicle had hit an overhanging branch from a large tree. The branch came crashing down on the road in front of us; Sitka spun round and shot off back down the road. Fortunately, he now knew he was better off waiting for me to go and 'rescue' him so never went far away before he realised he'd left me behind.

There was a notice I must have missed on our way south pointing towards a small cottage on the roadside saying, 'Cats this way' then as we passed the cottage, I noticed it was called 'WITCH COTTAGE!'

It was nearly the end of October and the days were getting shorter. We were up near Cirencester and on a bridleway as it began to get dark. There was no room to camp on the track but we came to an empty barn alongside the bridleway so we went in and spent the night there, but I couldn't help feeling guilty going into someone's property without their permission.

We were back onto the same route we had travelled south on, so I didn't have to keep referring to maps which was just as well, as the weather had turned into a wet spell which seemed reluctant to go away. Each time I listened to the weather forecast on my little radio, yet more rain was to come. The leaves were beginning to fall off the trees and cover the sides of the roads.

I could hear a motorbike ahead of us. It had to be coming towards us as the sound got louder and louder. If it was one of those speeding ones we had better get out of the way. But before we could get off the road it came flying round the bend ahead of us, swerved to the far side of the narrow road to avoid us then skidded on the wet leaves.

The motorbike ended up on its side with the rider thrown across the road. Tinker was ahead of us and fled on up the road. Russet had been tired so had asked to be up in his saddlebag. As the motorbike fell, Sitka

swung round and Russet fell out of his saddlebag as all the packs slipped sideways and ended up under Sitka's belly.

The motorbike rider got up and appeared to be none the worse apart from being covered in mud and wet leaves so I left him trying to get his motorbike upright and caught Sitka. There was nothing for it but to try to undo all the straps, buckles and girth then let all the packs and the saddle drop to the ground. At least it wasn't raining at the time so nothing got wet. Tinker came cautiously back to join us and Russet was none the worse. He even started to do his yapping as I began putting the saddle back onto Sitka as if we were just getting ready to set off for the day.

It was November 1st by the time we got back into Derbyshire to stay with my sister near Buxton for a few days, before doing the last lap home.

Sitka enjoyed a few days rest while I explored some of the local footpaths with the dogs. Tinker had plenty of energy but Russet wasn't so sure he wanted to come with us. He would watch us start off then decide he would rather stay behind and rest with Sitka.

The weather got colder with sleet and some snow later when we left Buxton. Up through the Goyt Valley – all very beautiful but it was cold and wet, made worse by the wind. After staying in my sister's house and sleeping in a warm bed it took some time adapting to being back in a tent in such cold November weather.

We spent one night back in the cowshed sleeping opposite the row of cattle tied up in stalls where every time they had a poo it splattered on the concrete behind them and bits splashed across and landed on my sleeping bag. I had to keep hiding my face down it to avoid being hit. I pulled the waterproof groundsheet over me but it kept slipping off every time I moved.

Another night I was in a hayshed where the wind kept blowing through the gaps near the roof sending dust and cobwebs off the rafters down onto us.

We were able to get onto more bridleways once into the North Yorkshire Dales with plenty of rabbits for Tinker and Russet to chase. It was while

picnicking one fine day when both terriers chased a rabbit down a burrow nearby, when I really noticed how much Tinker had grown over our eight-week trip to Devon. Russet was the first to start digging down the rabbit burrow then Tinker joined him and soon both were half down the hole with their bums sticking out. It was then that I realised both looked the same size and realised how much Tinker had grown. I had always had a suspicion the Tinker wasn't really a Jack Russell. It now looked more obvious a collie had got in there somehow. Her markings were that of a collie but the docked tail made her look like a terrier. Now her legs had grown longer and, apart from the docked tail, her body had more of a collie look. She had also got a bit too big for her saddlebag before we got to Devon, so while in Paignton I had extended it by letting out the sides, but now she was bulging more out of the top of her saddlebag and not looking very comfortable; I also had trouble getting her into her saddlebag. Her longer back legs didn't fold up enough to let her slip down into it. After years of experience of getting into a saddlebag Russet had the knack of reversing into it as he folded his back legs up so he could slide down into it and looked relaxed and comfortable.

We were well north of Hebden Bridge and the rain was pouring down. As we were passing a row of semi-detached cottages, the water from all the rain was running down the road into the entrance of one of them. A man was frantically digging to try and divert the water from entering his back door. An elderly lady was peering out of the window of the next cottage. She saw me then began to wave and I could see she was trying to tell me something but I couldn't make out what she was saying. Then she pointed to her door and I waited till she came out. I recognised her as the lady with the Alsatian dog I had met out walking in the area twice before. "You're not camping out in this are you?" she called then invited me in for a mug of tea. I tied Sitka up on her gate when she called out "Where are your dogs?" I lifted the front of the waterproof sheet covering Sitka's packs and the saddle and two faces peered out. "Bring them in with you!" she said so I let them out of their saddlebags and the three of us followed her into her cottage to find she was speaking to someone on her telephone. "Yes, I'll tell her," I heard her say. "I've just rung the farmer – you can put the pony in the field in front of my cottage for the night then you and the dogs can sleep on the settee in the living room for the night," she explained as she made the tea.

As it was so cold and wet outside I gratefully accepted what she said but where would I put all the wet soggy saddlebags and camping gear? The cottage was tiny and I couldn't bring them into it. We would be tripping over them, but she must have already thought about it and explained she had an old van across the road from her cottage – I could unload all my things off Sitka and put them all in it for the night.

I finished my mug of tea, left my dogs in her kitchen and went out to see to Sitka. It was so wet and bitterly cold outside. I heaved all the packs into the back of the old van then wrapped Sitka up in the waterproof sheet and led him to the field. The grass was good. His head went down straight away so I left him and went back in the cottage, glad to go inside again.

We chatted away then had some supper and by 9 o'clock all I wanted to do was go to sleep, but my host told me she only really woke up in the evenings! As she chatted, she must have seen me nodding off to sleep as I struggled in vain to stay awake. "Would you like a bath?" she said. That sounded like a good idea so I said "Yes, I would love one."

She led me upstairs to a tiny bathroom then got out a candle as she explained there was no electric light upstairs. In the corner was a large 'bucket' with a lid on it "That is an Elsan toilet but I don't use it unless I have to because it has to be carried down stairs and emptied into the council wagon that comes once a week for all of us here to empty our toilets into."

The bath was tiny and she explained that the water ran out into an outside drain by the roadside. I had my bath then was shown the bed settee in the living room. After taking the dogs out for a quick pee, I went back into the cottage and into the living room, then was handed a bucket "You use that to pee in, then tip it into the outside drain by the roadside in the morning" she explained, then left me with Russet and Tinker to make ourselves comfortable. I could hear the rain outside beating on the windows as I drifted off to sleep.

Next morning, I woke as daylight appeared through the window and got up to see if I could see Sitka. It wasn't raining, but there was a biting cold wind. There was Sitka grazing peacefully, his waterproof sheet still wrapped round him. As time passed, there was no sign of my host so eventually I decided to make myself a mug of coffee. She had shown me where the coffee was the night before after asking me if I liked tea or coffee in the morning; we both agreed we preferred coffee to wake us up. I finished my drink and still no sign of my host so I decided to go upstairs and take her a mug of coffee. I got to her bedroom door and called out to see if she was awake and said I had a coffee for her.

There was a grunt and a groan then the door opened and a figure stood there looking as if she was still asleep but she managed to hold the mug I gave her and said, "I'll be down soon." She was down soon but still didn't look quite awake.

I went to get Sitka in from the field and led him up to the old van. The wind was so cold my hands went numb as I tried to get him packed up. My fingers wouldn't work properly to do up the various buckles and straps. It took a long time before I was ready to call the dogs and say thank you and goodbye.

"Make sure you come and see me next time you are down this way," she called out as we went down the road. I was trying to walk briskly to get warmed up but Sitka wasn't having it. He was full of wet grass and had no intention of stepping out more quickly. Tinker was away ahead of us; she seemed to recognise the way from when we came south or maybe it was just by chance she was going ahead the right way!

Russet wasn't so full of energy. The two of us accepted Sitka's plod, plod pace even though I was trying to persuade him to walk faster all the time.

Later it started to rain and it began to get dark. We got a great welcome from Veronica who I first met on that first trip with Sitka some fourteen years earlier, so we had another night inside.

Our next night was at Linton with Helen; the 91-year-old artist who painted the most beautifully detailed pictures of wild flowers she found and knew so well in her area. She always seemed delighted to have someone to chat to nonstop about her favourite area called Grasswoods, near Grassington, and thought the clutter I made in her kitchen, with all the packs and camping gear, was very amusing.

She had a big old-fashioned camera that she placed on a tripod to take a photograph of Sitka all packed up and ready to leave in the morning; quite a complicated ritual which took up a bit of time before we could leave. Fortunately, over all the years we have stayed there, the mornings when we have been ready to leave have been fine so Helen has been able to get her camera out and set it up on its tripod to take a photograph of us by her cottage.

Our night in Helen's cottage was the last night in a bed until we got home. We had some very cold nights in the tent and having to pack up then get everything onto Sitka's back with frozen hands in the morning.

I was always glad to be going up and over steep Yorkshire Dales hillsides after setting off in the morning as it was the best way of getting warmed up, even if I had to drag a reluctant pack pony who refused to walk any faster.

Our last night was in a small sheepshed in Weardale belonging to a farmer in Westgate. The rain was beating down on the tin sheets on the roof, but the dogs and I were warm and comfortable inside. I had pulled some hay out of the hayrack at one end to put on the floor for the dogs to sit on before I got my sleeping bag out so they would dry off a bit. Suddenly I realised I had pulled a hedgehog out as well. It must have been hibernating in the hay. With two handfuls of hay to protect my hands from its prickly spines I picked it up and put it back in the hayrack. It gave a few groaning sounds then made the most revolting smell which I kept smelling all night.

Next morning was dry but very cold. My feet in cold boots refused to get warm even climbing up a very steep hill out of Westgate and over to Rookhope. Over the next hill and into Bay Bridge, my feet still felt so cold they ached. I saw a dead gorse bush down by the river so we stopped there and I managed to pull up the dead gorse out of the ground without getting my hands full of its sharp prickles, then broke it up by standing on it, placed some other dead wood on top of it, then lit the gorse which flared up quickly so I soon had a good fire going. I got my boots off and then put my feet by the fire so steam was rising from my socks and my feet were getting warm. The socks had to stay on my feet – if I had taken them off, they would not have gone on again and I had no more dry ones to put on.

Warm feet in warm wet socks aren't so bad as cold feet in cold wet socks. So, with warm wet feet in warm wet socks, back in cold wet boots, we set off again and got home as more rain came but it didn't matter anymore. We were back home.

ABOUT JANE

It was on a sunny September day in 2020 when Jane Dotchin, pack pony Diamond and terrier Dinky were walking near Tyndrum in the Scottish Highlands when she stopped to chat with the owner of the nearby holiday lodges, who recorded their conversation. Within days her story went viral resulting in over 40,000 views on Facebook and attracting media attention worldwide.

Born near Hexham in Northumberland in 1940, Jane, a very experienced horse rider, opened the Plover Hill Riding School in 1962. Jane had bred and successfully shown Fell ponies for many years. She started on her Spring and Autumn journeys in 1971, recording her adventures in illustrated diaries.

Fifty years after her first expeditions the British Horse Society awarded Jane the Exceptional Achievement Award for 'a notable triumph against the odds, showing determination, courage and sportsmanship'.

This book covers her trips from 1984 to 1987 when she travelled north to the Scottish Highlands and as far south to Devon.

Jane's new book 'More Journeys with a Pack Pony 1988 - 1994' is also available from Wagtail Press.

www.wagtailpress.uk